Milovaig Books

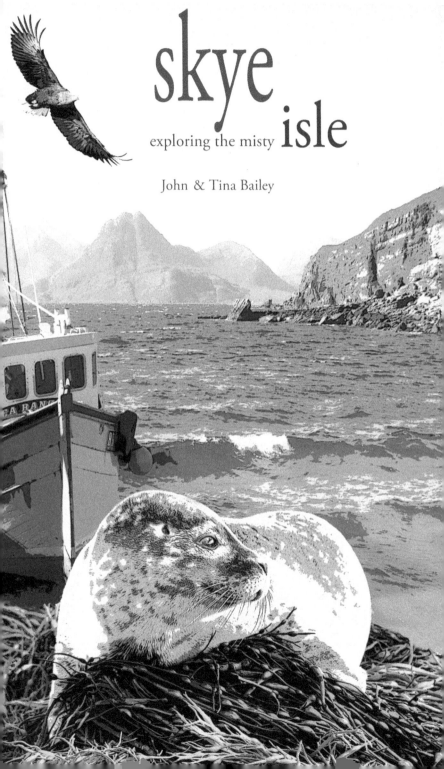

skye
exploring the misty isle

John & Tina Bailey

ACKNOWLEDGEMENTS

Inspiration for the completion of Skye (Exploring The Misty Isle) has not only come from the beautiful, awe-inspiring landscape but also from the numerous islanders that I have come to know. Many have provided me with a great awareness of the beauty and diversity of this magical island, a place where traditional values are still a part of everyday life.

I would like to thank each and every one that has taken time to reminisce about the island's past and present. I would especially like to acknowledge the following for their contribution and help in what has been a thoroughly rewarding experience. The peat-cutting process was admirably explained by Mr Jackson of Dunvegan, who took time out to demonstrate the craft of the peat cutter. My grateful thanks go to Gerry Akroyd MBE and the Skye Mountain Rescue Team for the detailed information and images supplied by Alan Law. My appreciation goes out to Jonathan MacDonald at The Skye Museum of Island Life Kilmuir, who provided the comprehensive details on the museum its history and for allowing the images to be reproduced for the book. A special acknowledgement must go to Hugh MacLeod of MacLeod, 30th Clan Chief of Dunvegan for the detailed text to ensure accuracy from Dunvegan Castle and for supplying the original photographs used to portray the castle images, and not least taking time out to write the foreword. A note of thanks must also go to the boatmen at Dunvegan Castle for the highly informative trip around the loch to visit the seal colonies; their knowledge is second to none and provides a unique opportunity for stunning photography.

As with my previous publications special thanks go to Tina, who has spent immeasurable hours travelling to capture the prefect scene, and has contributed to a good deal of the images*, and last but not least to Nick again for his contributions and helping with the equipment on some of the longer trails.

*The images used to illustrate the book have been taken from original photographs to recapture the bygone days of travel, a theme that was widely expressed in many travel posters promoting holiday destinations during the mid twentieth century.

Poster art courtesy of Milovaig Designs.

CONTENTS

FOREWORD

The Isle of Skye attracts increasing numbers of visitors each year. The magnetic attraction of the island is derived from the majestic grandeur of its land and seascapes, its history and the rich cultural legacy of its people. Together they provide the perfect antidote for those in search of a respite from the pressures of the modern world.

Although much has changed since two of its earliest visitors, Dr Johnson and James Boswell, made their celebrated tour of the Hebrides in 1773, there is a timeless quality which pervades the island.

As one old adage goes, 'Time on Skye is not the time you go by, but the time you remember'.

In his journal, Boswell remarked that they were 'sometimes relieved by a view of branches of the sea, that universal medium of connection amongst mankind and the wild, moorish, hilly and craggy appearances which gave a rude magnificence to the scene'.

That magnificent landscape which has inspired generations of writers, artists, climbers and walkers remains one of the few places in Europe where nature and not man is in control. It is a place where one can access a unique and solitary connection with the natural world.

John & Tina Bailey's informative and well-researched book, Skye, provides an insight into the magical places to explore and savour on the Isle of Skye.

Hugh MacLeod of MacLeod
Dunvegan Castle & Gardens Collection
Isle of Skye

KYLERHEA
OVER THE SEA TO SKYE
Ferry service operating between Easter and October

INTRODUCTION

In the 1920s and the 1930s H V Morton undertook a tour of Scotland driving a Bullnose Morris concluding on Skye where he believed Skye was 'The strangest place in the British Isles'. Looking for the perfect vista on which to end his journey, Morton wasn't disappointed rewarded with magnificent views from the lofty summits of the Cuillin.
H V Morton author of In Search of Scotland 1892 -1979

The Isle of Skye (Scottish Gaelic: An t-Eilean Sgitheanach or Eilean a' Cheó) is the largest and most northerly of the Inner Hebrides a group of islands bordering the north-west coast of Scotland. It is an island of immense contrasts, ranging from the magnificent rugged coast with cliffs that rise 1,000 ft from the sea, tranquil sea lochs with jagged shorelines that continue deep inland, vast rolling moor land and the extraordinary geological features of the Trotternish Ridge. The culmination of the diverse landscape is complete with the majestic Cuillin, rising over 3,000 ft above sea level. It is the continually shifting light creating an extraordinary variety of dramatic moods complementing the beautiful landscape, together with the islands sometimes brutal history and way of life, that has drawn me to explorer and share this wonderful island called Skye, alas not in a Bullnose Morris.

Our journey begins in the south at the nearest point to the mainland, Kylerhea, where you can still come over the sea to Skye in the traditional way. Skye has remarkably differing regions, and these can be categorised as the southern peninsula of Sleat, sometimes referred to as the garden of Skye, Minginish that encompasses the Cuillin, Duirinish, Waternish and Trotternish all major promontories. A main road heads north from the bridge at Kyleakin to the Island capital Portree, straddling the coast and moorland eventually reaching Uig, a major port to the Western Isles.

The Strathaird peninsula is the first port of call, found west of Broadford where a single track road continues under the shadow of Bla Bhienn to reach the shore at Elgol. The Cuillin, 12 Munros (peaks above 3,000 ft), have been described as the most untamed and scenic mountain range in Britain; when viewed from the shore at Elgol no one would dispute that statement. It is a majestic mountain range that I have been told should always be referred to as just the Cuillin. The Cuillin are made up of the Black Cuillin (the main ridge and Bla Bhienn) and the Red Cuillin, the smaller rounded hills that are separated by Glen Sligachan.

To the north-west are the regions of Durinish and Minginish, impressive peninsulas of rolling moorland and rugged, sparsely inhabited coastline. Durinish is home to the distinctive flat-topped mountains of MacLeods Tables. The area is steeped in history, where the Highland clearances have had a major influence on the peoples and the landscape. The north-west is home to Dunvegan Castle, the ancestral home of Clan MacLeod, set on a rocky outcrop on Loch Dunvegan with the tranquil waters providing a safe haven for a colony of seals.

Skye's most northerly peninsula, Trotternish is a geologist's delight with its vast inland cliff running for over 20 miles, bedecked with mysterious pinnacles and peaks, the peninsula culminating with the spectacular cliffs above Rubha Hunish, the northernmost point of Skye. The scenery of Skye is extraordinary, and so is the islands history. We learn about Bonnie Prince Charlie and how, despite a huge bounty on his head, he was never betrayed by the Highlanders. The Highland Clearances and how the crofters eventually acquired security of tenure. I have included brief details of eight walks that allows one to experience some of Skye's remote areas only accessible on foot. Weather conditions always need to be considered before setting out. Care is needed for the higher areas of Trotternish and the Cuillin, as mists can descend even on the clearest of days, making navigation difficult.

It is the dramatic landscape Skye has to offer, the fascinating history and the constantly changing moods of the weather and light that will live long in your memory should you visit, and leaves one with a constant desire to return.

DRIVING SINGLE TRACK ROADS

Driving on these roads brings back memories of a bygone era but requires thought and concentration. There are usually plenty of passing places and these are marked with a sign, but unless you want to make yourself very unpopular remember that these are passing and not parking places.

The trick on single-track roads is to drive with a combination of consideration and assertiveness. In an ideal world vehicles approaching one another should adjust their speeds so as to meet at a passing place, that way neither waits for the other, and both proceed at best speed. Bear in mind that if the passing place is on the right and you reach it first, stop on the left side of the road opposite the passing place, do not be tempted into pulling across to the right.

Keep a close watch on your mirror. If someone comes up behind you they are travelling the road faster than you are, you should use a passing place to pull over and let them through. This is more than simple courtesy as some of the the road signs emphasise this point.

OVER THE SEA TO SKYE

Speed, bonnie boat, like a bird on the wing, Onward! the sailors cry;
Carry the lad that's born to be King, Over the sea to Skye.
Loud the winds howl, loud the waves roar, Thunderclaps rend the air;
Baffled our foes stand by the shore, Follow they will not dare.
Though the waves leap, soft shall ye sleep, Ocean's a royal bed:
Rocked in the deep, Flora will keep, Watch by your weary head.
Many's the lad fought on that day, Well the Claymore could wield:
When the night came silently lay, Dead in Culloden's field.
Burned are their homes, exile and death, Scatter the loyal men;
Yet ere the sword cool in the sheath, Charlie will come again.

The Scottish folk song tells the story of the escape of Charles Edward Stuart, 'Bonnie Prince Charlie', from Uist to Skye after his defeat at Culloden in 1746. Charlie, now a fugitive, was tracked down to South Uist, where Flora MacDonald had agreed to help smuggle the Prince to Skye in a small boat, dressed as her maid Betty Burke. The song was first published by Boulton and MacLeod in 1884. Miss Annie MacLeod first heard the Gaelic air 'Cuchag nan Craobh' being sung during a boat trip across Loch Coruisk by her rowers; she wrote down the music and Sir Harold Boulton later penned the lyrics.

There is uncertainty as to when the first crossing to Skye would have been established, but the shortest route is to be found here between the mainland, just under 2 miles north of Glenelg and kylerhea on Skye. The Kyle Rhea is a mere 600 yards wide at this point and would have been used by drovers taking their Highland cattle on the long journey from the Hebrides south to the Lowlands. It is said that some cattle would be swept away, only to make landfall on the shore at Glenelg.

Looking across to the mainland from the shores of Skye at Kylerhea.

The road to Glenelg began life as a military road and is still noted today as such on OS maps, constructed to reach the barracks at Bernera, now a ruin dating from the 18th century. The present road still follows much of the old route. The crossing from the mainland to kylerhea was the popular route to Skye until the Victorian period of railway building opened up the Highlands, with the line eventually reaching Kyle of Lochalsh in November 1897. A main ferry port was then established at Kyleakin and remained the gateway to Skye until the opening of the bridge in 1995.

The present car and passenger ferry at Kylerhea began in 1934 and continues operating between Easter and October. Today, the ferry service is run by The Isle of Skye Ferry Community Interest Company using the only turntable ferry of its type in Britain, providing a traditional and romantic journey across the sea to Skye.

Sleat is the most southern peninsula, often overlooked on the visitors' journey to the mountainous region of the Cuillin. During late summer, the wild beauty of the quiet roads and coastal fringes of Skye are adorned by swathes of the brightly coloured orange-red flowers of the Montbretia, their display enhanced dancing in the gentlest of breezes. Originating from South Africa, having a variety of eight species, Montbretia was named after the French botanist Conqebert de Montbret (1780-1801).

Montbretia colonise best in coastal locations. Although naturalised throughout Britain for gardeners, Montbretia is ideal for growing in herbaceous borders, with the flowers excellent for cutting. The plant is hardy enough to survive as far north as the Hebrides. Forming dense clumps with new corms continually produced below ground, the plants soon take a firm foothold on their location.

STRATHAIRD

The small port of Elgol, as with many locations on Skye, has served in the past as the only route for supplies in and out of the area before the construction of the single-track road from Broadford. The road twists and turns for over 14 miles, skirting the shore of Loch Slapin under the shadow of Blaven (Bla Bheinn), ahead of reaching the shore at Elgol, adding to the remote feel of the Strathaird peninsula. The Millennium stone that stands proud above Dunvegan was taken from the shores of Strathaird. The single-track road provides some notable views to contrast the coastal areas, meandering as it does along the valley of Strath Suardal to Loch Slapin, in particular at Loch Cill Chriosd. The ruined church at Cill Chriosd, (Christ's Church) dates from the early 1500s, but it is believed an earlier structure stood on this site dating from mediaeval times. The church served as the parish church for Strathaird up until the mid 1800s.

A short distance from Cill Chriosd Church we find the shallow reed-filled waters of Loch Cill Chriosd beneath the slopes of Dearg Bheag, often reflected in its calm waters. Legend has it that these waters were home to an evil spirit that poisoned the waters, and anyone who washed in or drank the waters would succumb to harm. The waters became blessed from a visit by St Columba, and from that time on the waters were believed to be 'good for all'. St Columba, who had visited Skye during the 6th century, was also known as Colum Cille, meaning 'dove of the church'. A Gaelic Irish missionary monk, St Columba spread Christianity among the Picts during the Early Mediaeval Period. He is predominantly linked with the northern most part of Skye, although much better known for his association with the island of Iona.

BLAVEN

Beyond Loch Cill Chriosd the single-track road continues the length of the valley floor to reach Torrin, close to the shore of Loch Slapin, a picturesque sea loch under the shadow of Bla Bheinn. Pronounced Blah-yen and often referred to as Blaven, the mountain mass is an outlier of the main Cuillin ridge, providing a most striking backdrop to the loch when viewed from the southern shores. Blaven is one of 12 Munros on Skye, separated from the main Cuillin ridge by Glen Sligachan. The term Munro is synonymous with Scotland, named after the early leader of Scottish mountaineering Sir Hugh Munro, who set out to survey every peak above 3000 ft in 1891. Sir Hugh died before he could conquer all the peaks. Just two remained, one here on Skye, the Inaccessible Pinnacle, and a lesser peak in the Cairngorms eventually downgraded in a survey carried out in 1981. The illustrious feat was secured by the Rev A E Robertson in 1901, 12 years after his first conquest. He did, though, complete them in what was described as an efficient manner, linking the peaks as opposed to a separate climb for each as Sir Hugh had undertaken. From a geologist's perspective, the Cuillin consists mainly of Gabbro and sheets of Dolerite, giving it a distinctive appearance. Gabbro is a hard rock, a delight for climbers as it provides good adhesion, but care is needed in the Cuillin as navigation by a compass can be unreliable.

BLAVEN

The classic view of Bla Bheinn, across the blue waters of Loch Slapin. Blaven is the
most easterly peak of the Black Cuillin. Separated from the main Cuillin ridge by
Glen Sligachan, Blaven at 3,044 ft is one of twelve Munros on Skye

KILMARIE to CAMASUNARY WALK
Distance 6 miles with an estimated time of 3.5 to 4.5 hours.

The only access to Camasunary is on foot, adding to the remoteness of this wonderful, wild treasure. The only signs of habitation are the two houses standing on the strand of green sward, dwarfed by the mountains of the Black Cuillin. The setting is enhanced by the expanse of sand and pebbles, constantly shifting from the pounding waters of Loch Scavaig.

The route begins just south-west of the small settlement of Kilmarie on the B8083 at grid reference 545 172, where road side parking can be found. The first part of the walk follows the Land Rover track built by the army in 1968 to allow better emergency access to the south-east of the Cuillin. The track made it as far as Camasunary but has not been well maintained, helping to preserve the area's remoteness. It was proposed to continue the track around the coast to Loch Coruisk, destroying the Bad Step. The idea was met with a chorus of disapproval from mountaineers, who prevented further progress.

The land is now owned by the John Muir Trust. Founded in 1983, the trust is dedicated to the protection of wild land for both nature and people. The trust also owns Kilmarie House, purchased from Ian Anderson, a member of the seventies rock band Jethro Tull, in 1994.

Cross the road to go through the gate where a plaque confirms the work of the army in 1968. The inviting track heads west-north-west, with the early section a moderate steady rise following the contours of the land. Close to the shielings the track drops to ford a burn, then begins to gain height. Go through the gate to continue upward, passing a cairn. At this point the track becomes rougher and considerably steeper for the next mile. The rewards for the ascent are breathtaking views unfolding as you reach the pass of Am Mam. Ahead are the Cuillin, with the jagged peak of Sgurr nan Gillean in full view.

After about twenty minutes walking Loch Scavaig and Camas Fhionnairigh finally come into view, with the dwelling on the strand giving a true perspective to the scale of the scene. The awe-inspiring view encompasses the Cuillin ridge with the distant Garsbheinn, Sgurrr na Stri and Camasunary. The route to Camasunary is now clear to see. As you begin to descend, take the stony track down on your left - the route continuing ahead would lead you to Loch na Creitheach and eventually Glen Sligachan. The track now drops down taking a series of twists and turns to cross the river Abhainn nan Leac. The crystal clear cool waters of Abhainn nan Leac emerge high on the slopes of Bla Bheinn cascading just under 2 miles to Loch Scavaig. The course is constantly interrupted as the waters tumble over several rocky outcrops creating miniature waterfalls and numerous magical glistening pools on its journey to the sea.

After heavy rains, the tranquil pools become impressive torrents. The first dwelling you see is privately owned, while at the far end of the beach is Camasunary bothy. Beyond the bothy, the Abhainn Camas Fhionnairigh flows into the sea. The river can be forded at low tide close to the remains of the old bridge should you wish to continue your journey into Loch Coruisk via the Bad Step. The bridge, part of the original plan to continue the track to Loch Coruisk, was soon destroyed by the forces of nature, with the Bad Step remaining intact.

What is certain is that you may possibly yearn to spend some considerable time here to take in the extraordinary tranquillity and feeling of seclusion of this beautiful setting. The panorama from the shoreline out across Loch Scavaig takes in Rum some 12 miles distant and the much closer Isle of Soay, once a base for the author of *Ring of Bright Water*, Gavin Maxwell.

The old Scandinavian name for Soay, Sauda-ey means 'Island of sheep'. Although a satellite of Skye, Soay is sometimes considered to be part of the Small Isles. The islanders were evacuated to Mull during 1953. Beyond lies the small island of Canna, the furthermost of the Small Isles from the mainland. During the summer months the strand is bedecked with cotton grass and bog myrtle, whilst sporadic clumps of fox glove can be seen striving to keep a foothold on the heather-clad hillside.

The way back to the car park is taken by retracing your steps up the steep, twisting and turning track to the pass of Am Mam. You are, nevertheless, rewarded with equally spectacular views as the outward journey had provided. Once at Am Mam, the remainder of the route is an easy but pleasing descent following the Land Rover track back to the car park.

Our journey now continues eastward along the single-track road with widespread views opening south-east across to Loch Eishort and the Sleat peninsula, together with the distant mountains of the mainland beyond. After a distance of 3 miles, the road begins to descend in a series of twists and turns, to arrive on the coast at the scattered settlement and port of Elgol.

The Bothy Camasunary with the Cuillin as an inspirational backdrop.
Left to right: Squrr Hain, Marsco and Bla Bheinn.

ELGOL
Travel to Skye for one of the best views in Britain
Alfred Wainwright once stood on these shores and proclaimed that it was the best view in Britain

ELGOL

The small crofting settlements of Elgol and Torrin were held by Clan MacKinnon, who fashioned a strong allegiance to the Jacobite uprising aimed at restoring James Stuart to the throne led by James VIII's son Prince Charles Edward Stuart, the 'Young Pretender' or 'Bonnie Prince Charlie'.

Elgol is said to have been the last hiding place on Skye for the Prince before his escape to the mainland in 1746.

In 1745 Prince Charles Edward Stuart, aged 23, sailed to Scotland intent on raising an army of Highland Clans to restore the exiled Kings to the thrones of England, Scotland and Ireland, the 45' Jacobite rebellion.

His forces were to take Perth, Edinburgh and Carlisle, but on reaching Derby without support promised from France and only limited cooperation from English Jacobites the Prince was forced to retreat back to Scotland. Outnumbered, the forces were defiant, eventually being heavily defeated when they met an army led by his cousin William Duke of Cumberland on Culloden Moor on 16 April 1746. By this time the Prince had a bounty on his head for £30,000, an enormous sum remembering this was over 250 years ago. Despite the bounty, the Prince was never betrayed by the Highlanders, who believed he would return to fight again.

After his escape from Uist to Skye, Bonnie Prince Charlie, still being pursued, eventually arrived at Elgol, having returned to Skye from Raasay. Captain John MacKinnon rowed the Prince across the Sound of Sleat to the mainland, aiding the Prince in his quest to seek safe refuge in France. Charles spent most of the remainder of his life in Italy, having been born in Rome.

Legend goes that the Prince gave MacKinnon a gift for his efforts, a recipe of his personal medicinal elixir. The recipe remained lost within the MacKinnon family for over a century until being produced locally as An Dram Buidheach, later to become the world famous liquor, 'Drambuie'. Like most of the Highlands, Elgol and Torrin were to later witness a dreadful exodus of the population during the infamous Highland Clearances.

Penning the right words to describe a view can at times be a quandary, as the trend can be to exaggerate the splendour of the occasion, but here from the shore at Elgol that could never be the case. The view out across Loch Scavaig north-east into the heart of the Cuillin cannot be equalled and can genuinely be described as sublime. Alfred Wainwright once stood on these shores and proclaimed that it was the best view in Britain, and very few if any would disagree with the great man's sentiments.

A visit to the heart of the Cuillin provides one with a pleasant conundrum: two options come to the fore, providing the visitor with equally impressive experiences that will live long in the memory. The more demanding of the two necessitates a start at Sligachan, walking the track that begins crossing the old pack-horse bridge. A long-distance track runs through Glen Sligachan, following under the shadow of Marsco then traverses the ridge of Druim Hain below the summit of Sgurr Hain. The route continues, descending from this point to reach the stepping stones crossing the Scavaig River to reach Loch Coruisk, a distance of over 7 miles.

Unless you are equipped to spend a night wild camping, you will need to be prepared to return to Sligachan by the same route, therefore planning of the walk is essential.

Sufficient food and drink would need to be carried, as this is a truly remote wild place, and the route should only be attempted by experienced hill walkers, who can complete 15 miles of rough terrain in a single day. The easier option, but none the less rewarding, is to take one of the boat trips from the jetty at Elgol, a captivating journey passing colonies of seals on the rocky shores of the tiny islets that adorn the loch.

As you are drawn towards Loch Coruisk, the heather-clad mountains begin to take on their true appearance as giants rising abruptly from the sea. Crossing the Loch, it is easy to allow your mind to drift back to the 1870s, to the time when Annie MacLeod was taking a boat trip on the loch, and hear the beautifully haunting lyrics and music of The Skye Boat Song.

The classic view afforded from the shore at Elgol has to be one of the finest in Britain. The splendour of the Cuillin rise abruptly from the sea to their lofty heights above 3,000 ft. Loch Coruisk lies at the foot of Druim nan Ramh seen emanating from the main ridge in the centre of the Cuillin.

As we set out from Elgol to Loch Coruisk, the Island offshore to the west is Soay, worth a detour into the small harbor on its north-west shore to view the remains of a long abandoned shark fishing industry. In 1945 the author Gavin Maxwell establish a shark fishing factory on Soay, having bought the island from the MacLeods of Dunvegan. His attempt to turn it into a commercial venture would finally fail in 1948. The huge carcases would have been hauled ashore from the small harbour, with the livers used for oil, but the process required steam. A railway engine was brought by rail to Mallaig, finally reaching Soay by boat.

The true history of Gavin Maxwell's adventures on Soay are told in his book *Harpoon at a Venture.*

Loch Coruisk has been described as the most spectacularly sited loch in the British Isles, set in the basin of Coir Uisg. A closer look at Coire an Uaigneis, and Sgurr a Mhadaidh on the main ridge make it clear to see why they are referred to as the Black Cuillin. During the ice age, immense glaciers would have gouged out the great corries, leaving behind the sheer ridges and peaks that make up the unique character of the Cuillin.

This inland loch provides a route deep into the eastern Cuillin and the Inaccessible Pinnacle, affectionately known as the Inn Pin. The track from Camasunary provides a shorter option than the route from Sligachan, initially following the Land Rover track from Kilmarie, a total distance of 5 miles, but presents somewhat of tough test, as it requires negotiating The Bad Step. The route skirts the western slopes of Sgurr na Stri, where a slab of rock curves into the sea and requires some scrambling above deep open water.

A small jetty in Loch na Cuilce serves as a convenient stopping-off point for the boats from Elgol. Set close to the jetty is Loch Coruisk Memorial Hut, built in 1959 as a memorial for two young climbers who lost their lives whilst climbing on Ben Nevis. The hut is in the care of the Junior Mountaineering Club of Scotland, used as a base for excursions into the Cuillin.

Gavin Maxwell established a shark fishing factory on Soay in 1945.

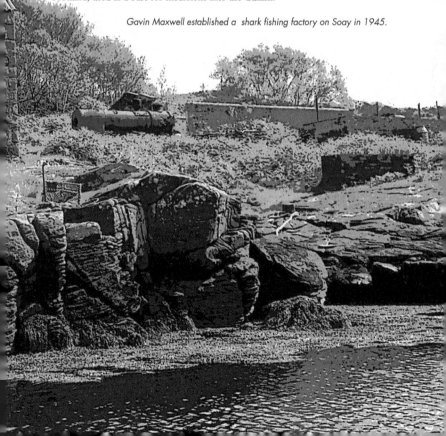

LOCH CORUISK

Described as the most spectacularly sited loch in the British Isles set in the basin of Coir Uisg. During the ice age immense glaciers gouged out the great corries leaving behind the sheer ridges and peaks

Our journey continues away from the awe-inspiring scenery of Loch Scavaig, returning under the shadow of Blaven to the village of Broadford, where we rejoin the main road running from Kyleakin to Uig. As we know, Kyleakin was the main gateway to Skye before the opening of the bridge in 1995, with a ferry service from Kyle of Lochalsh. The main route to the port of Uig, a distance of some 50 miles, starts just west of Kyleakin, hugging the coast at the foot of the mountains between Broadford and Sligachan. Magnificent coastal scenery is afforded, with views across The Inner Sound to Scalpay and Raasay. The road was built in the 1820s by Thomas Telford as part of the government's plans for road and bridge building in the Highlands.

Impressive waterfalls cascade alongside the road as it climbs through the glen between Beinn Dearg Mhor and Druim nan Cleochd. As the last snows of winter melt from the mountains, the waterfalls provide a spectacular sight accompanied by a thunderous sound. One such encounter is above Loch Ainort as the road begins to climb steeply, negotiating a sharp bend. Many tributaries feed Allt Coire nam Bruadaran, beginning their journey high upon the slopes of Marsco, cascading just over 2 miles to Eas a' Bhradain before entering Loch Ainort.

SLIGACHAN

As we approach Sligachan, the dominate shape of Glamaig, one of the Red Hills comes into full view, the road circumnavigating the eastern, northern and western slopes before entering Sligachan.

Glamaig, at 2,543 ft, was the site of a notable achievement in 1899 when Thapa a Ghurkha ran barefoot from Sligachan to the summit and back in 75 minutes. His feat was doubted by some, so completing the run again he somehow managed to achieve it in a remarkable time of 55 minutes. During July an annual race is now held, and Thapa's record stood proud until the 1980s.

The scenery at Sligachan does not disappoint. It is a most pleasing setting, with the Cuillin providing a constant changing backdrop for the old pack-horse bridge and one of the most popular routes into the Cuillin. The hotel at Sligachan was built as a coaching inn around 1830 and rapidly became a haven for early gentlemen climbers. The correct pronunciation for Sligachan, so I have been told, is 'Slig-a-han'. Glen Sligachan separates the loftier Black Cuillin from the more rounded Red Cuillin, with the exception of Blaven at 3,044 ft, one of the 12 Munros on Skye. The distinction of the highest peak belongs to Sgurr Alasdair at 3,259 ft, translated its meaning is the Peak of Alexander, named after Alexander Nicholson who made the first ascent in 1873. The ridge extends for over 6 miles, has 10,000 ft of ascent and is graded as 'very difficult rock climb'.

ISLE OF SKYE

As the last snows of winter melt from the mountains, waterfalls provide a
spectacular sight, accompanied by a thunderous sound.

SLIGACHAN
The Pack-horse Bridge

Marsco, standing over 2,350 ft, seen sporting its winter coat, creating a most delightful backdrop for the old pack-horse bridge. Sligachan became a haven for early gentlemen climbers with the advent of a coaching inn built around 1830.

H V Morton said of The Cuillin, *"It seems as if nature when she hurled the Coolins up into the light of the sun said. I will make mountains which shall be the essence of all that can be terrible in mountains. I will pack into them all the fearful shapes. Their scarred ravines, on which nothing shall grow, shall lead up to towering spires of rock, sharp splinters shall strike the sky along their mighty summits, and they shall be formed of rock unlike any other rock so that they will never look the same for very long, now blue, now grey, now silver, sometimes seeming to retreat or to advance, but always drenched in mystery and terrors".*

A classic Cuillin view is afforded from Sligachan, where a track to Glenbrittle passes the remote Altdearg House on route to Coir a Mhadaidh at the heart of the Cuillin. The peaks of Sgurr nan Gillen, Am Bastier and Sgurr Bastier dominant the skyline. Prevailing westerly winds and cloudy days on Skye will inevitably mean that the lofty Cuillin is obscured from view; however surreal conditions occur when high-level cloud and swirling mists form above and below the summits.

The dark summits seemingly appear from nowhere, only to fade away a few moments later, and the ridge with its many peaks takes on an eerie manifestation in complete contrast to clearer days that offer uninterrupted views of the entire ridge.

The Black Cuillin are the most spectacular and dangerous mountains in Britain. The higher peaks should only be attempted by experienced climbers, although the lower slopes will provide breathtaking mountain scenery without too much difficulty, providing you are fully prepared and equipped. Should you decide to venture to the loftier peaks and lack experience, then the prudent option would be to hire the services of a guide.

The variety of the rugged Cuillin scenery encompasses craggy peaks and picturesque waterfalls.

CUILLIN HILLS
ISLE OF SKYE
Winter comes early to the lofty summits

SKYE MOUNTAIN RESCUE TEAM

The visitor's book at the Sligachan Hotel records the first mountain rescue incident on Skye in 1870 when a man fell and died whilst descending Sgurr nan Gillean. Between the years of 1870 and 1930 there were three further fatalities recorded in the visitor's book. The years from 1930 onward were to witness increasing numbers of visitors to the mountains and with this came increasing incidents and fatalities. During the war years there was little mountaineering activity, but with visitors to the mountains increasing again during the 1950's the first volunteer rescue team was established on Skye. Jonacks MacKenzie, the Portree postman, led a team of local shepherds, ghillies and policemen. By this time the first RAF Search and Rescue helicopters were operating alongside the volunteers. In the 1960's Pete Thomas took over as Team Leader, a role he held for over a decade, and subsequently John MacLeod in 1971 for an interim year. John Macleod later received an MBE from the Queen for services to mountain rescue after serving as Skye Mountain Rescue Team Chairman for many years. In 1972 the current Team Leader, Gerry Akroyd, took on this role and continues in this post today. In January 2010 Gerry was awarded an MBE for services to mountain rescue in the Queen's New Years honours list.

The 35-strong members of the Skye Mountain Rescue Team are local men and women from all over the island who give up their time to assist walkers and climbers in a time of emergency. The team members are all volunteers and receive no payment or retainer fee. The team has two purpose-built huts, one in Glenbrittle and another at Sligachan which were built with the generous help of the Order of St. John; these act as base stations and control centres during rescues. The Skye Mountain Rescue Team is a registered charity, and their work is supported financially by a mixture of public donations, some grant aid from Mountain Rescue Scotland, toward training costs, support from other charities and fundraising to equip and run their team. When someone is in trouble on the hills the police are called, and if it requires a mountain rescue callout, Skye Mountain Rescue Team are alerted by telephone to meet at a specific point. Team members receive regular training in skills such as first aid, navigation, rope-work, working with helicopters, and winter mountaineering. Members of the team provide a wealth of diverse skill, including a search and rescue dog handler (SARDA), a team doctor, rope access specialists and several mountain leaders and guides.

Mountain safety is paramount, and the Cuillin should not be underestimated. Always be prepared to turn back should mists begin to descend. Adequate clothing is essential and a good pair of mountain boots. Plenty of food and two litres of fluids should be carried to cover the unexpected. Before attempting to set out, ensure you are familiar with a good map and how to use it. A compass should be carried, but magnetic properties along the Cuillin ridge and in the corries can render them unreliable. You should always ensure someone knows your intended route and expected time of return. The Skye team carries and maintains a great deal of rescue equipment whicht has to be replaced on a regular basis when damaged or outdated.

The Skye Mountain Rescue Team has two main bases located at Sligachan and Glenbrittle, which were built with the generous help of the Order of St. John. These act as base stations and incident control centres during rescues.

MINGINISH

As we continue north-west from Sligachan, extended views of the Cuillin ridge open up from Glen Drynoch. Our next destination, Minginish, is home to Glenbrittle and Talisker Bay, both only accessible along single-track roads from the B8009 at Carbost. As we know, Glenbrittle is home to one of the two mountain rescue posts on *Skye* and for good reason; Glenbrittle is perhaps the most popular route for several excursions into the Cuillin. Hill walkers can, with care, access many of the lower slopes to marvel at the spectacular mountain scenery, without the need for scrambling, whilst experienced rock climbers continue to the loftier peaks.

The old farm buildings at the head of Gleann Oraid now showing signs of weathering, their dark red painted finish giving way to blue-grey and rusting hues now merging into the landscape, creating a striking foreground to The Cuillin.

TALISKER BAY WALK
Distance 6 miles with an estimated time of 3- 3.5 hours

Leaving behind the mountainous region of central Skye, we now discover an entirely different but equally magnificent landscape, one akin to what would be most people's perception of a remote island off the north-west coast of Scotland, a landscape of rolling moorland, rugged sea cliffs, prominent hills and beautiful glens. Preshal More stands more than 1000 ft overlooking Talisker and Gleann Oraid and is the dominant feature on this amble following the glen down to the sea, with the River Talisker close at hand. The walk begins by roadside parking at the top of Gleann Oraid at grid reference 353 304, taking care not to park in a passing place.

The route is a there-and-back walk and, if taken during spring through to summer, the moorland and cliffs are alive with an eye-catching display of wild flowers that at times reproduce a Dorset meadow. Vast swathes of wild hyacinths create a carpet of pale blue, while cottongrass with their hair like seed heads provide a continual display of dancing drifts of white, even in the slightest of breeze. As with most of Skye, the coastal fringes are awash with thrift, creating irregular patterns of deep to pale pink, with the often azure sea as a stunning backdrop. An overabundance of other wild flowers some unique to the Hebrides, can be seen growing in the most unusual of places, looking at their best set against the lush green moorland or contrasting deeply against a rocky outcrop. A most essential companion should be a pocket book on the wild flowers of Scotland. Continue to descend serene Gleann Oraid on the easy-going single track road until you reach the tiny settlement under the shadow of Preshal More. Take the track on the left heading towards the bay lined by a stone wall, trees and woodland. The stone walls and woodland are a haven for mosses and lichens, a rare setting on Skye. The track eventually passes Talisker House dating from the 1720s, the favourite residence of the MacLeods after Dunvegan Castle.

Talisker Bay was described as unlike any other area of Skye in the writings of James Boswell. In 1773 Dr Johnson, along with James Boswell, while touring The Hebrides spent time at Talisker House. Boswell wrote of Talisker: *"Talisker is a better place than one commonly finds in Skye. It is situated in a rich bottom. Before it is a wide expanse of sea, on each hand of which are immense rocks; and, at some distance to the sea, there are three columned rocks rising to sharp points. The billows break with prodigious force and noise on the coast of Talisker. There are here a good many well grown trees"*. The pair also spent time at Dunvegan Castle and Ullinish House. The previous year Thomas Pennant had completed his journey through the Highlands and Islands, of which Dr Johnson said of Pennant that he was the best traveller ever read. A clear path continues over the waters running from Sleadale Burn following towering cliffs on your left until reaching the shore. The beach is made up of large pebbles and a fusion of white and black sand. The tall cliffs to the north are enhanced by a picturesque waterfall fed from Loch an Sguirr Mhoir. The beach, with its grassy foreshore, is a most pleasant place to rest and observe 'the billows breaking with prodigious force' before the return journey back up through Gleann Oraid.

PRESHAL MORE   ISLE OF SKYE
Preshal More stands over 1000 ft high overlooking Gleann Oraid and Talisker

TALISKER BAY

Follow in the footsteps of James Boswell and Dr Johnson

LOCH HARPORT
ISLE OF SKYE

Loch Harport is a narrow loch, an ideal location for anglers when weather conditions are adverse.

DUN BEAG BROCH, STRUAN

Leaving Minginish behind, we now continue north, the A863 hugging the rugged coast for the majority of the next 9 miles before reaching Struan, the journey providing spectacular views of the coast, and as we glimpse back south the distant Cuillin remain a prominent feature. Heading toward Struan, two distinctive landmarks, MacLeod's Tables, firstly come into view and will dominate most of our journey through north-west Skye. At Struan we find the remains of Dun Beag Broch, regarded as one of the best preserved on Skye. Derived from Norse, Borg, meaning Fort, the broch was believed to have been built between 700BC and AD550. These massive dry stone structures were round in shape, with walls up to 12 feet thick, and many can be found throughout the Western and Northern Isles. The structure would almost certainly have been roofed, with the stone stairs built inside the double layer of walls.

Dun Beag Broch was visited in 1772 by author of *A Tour In Scotland,* Thomas Pennant. Their exact use remains shrouded in mystery; some believe they were built solely for defence while others say they were used for habitation, being early farm houses. Today the remaining walls are well preserved but would probably have stood up to 30 ft high, with the ground floor used for livestock and the upper levels for living being roofed over with wood and thatch. Commanding views are afforded over Loch Bracadale from Dun Beag Broch, adding to another theory of their use as beacons by Martin Martin, writing an account of his travels around The Hebrides during 1695. His book *A Description of the Western Isles of Scotland* first published in 1703, is said to have aided future travellers such as Thomas Pennant, James Boswell and Samuel Johnson. Massive blocks of stone were used in the construction of the dry-stone walls. During the years 1914 to 1920, Dun Beag was excavated, and it is debated that some rebuilding work could have taken place. Artefacts found during the excavations date from the Iron-Age and Viking times.

As we continue north the rolling treeless moorland landscape and coastal fringes of Duirinish, becomes dominated by the mystifying flat-toppedmountains of Healabhal Mhor standing over 1530 ft and the smaller looking though higher Healabhal Bheag, known locallyand detailed on OS mapping as MacLeod's Tables.

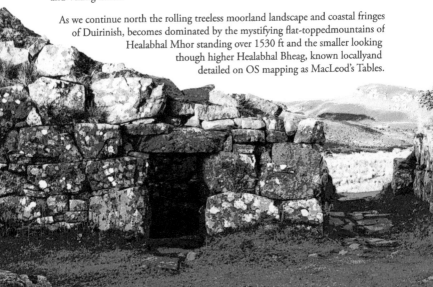

DUN BEAG BROCH
STRUAN

Previous page:
A section of the stone stairs built inside the double layer of walls remains well preserved today.

Officially called Harebell this delicate flower is known as
Bluebell in Scotland flowering during mid to late summer.

A small boat is a classic sight throughout Skye, sought out by artists and photographers, this classic one appearing to have withstood all that mother nature has presented over many years, nevertheless appearing sea-worthy and resolute.

ISLE OF SKYE
MacLeods Table (Healabhal Mhor)

MacLeod's Table North reflected in the tranquil waters of Loch Dunvegan, viewed from the shore at Dunvegan.

47

MACLEOD'S TABLES

Healabhal Mhor rises over 1530 ft above sea leve, while the smaller in mass Healabhal Bheag rises above 1600 ft, both appearing as if they have being sliced off by a giant and legend claims just that. It is said they were sliced off to provide a bed and table for St Columba. Another legend has it that the Ninth Chief of MacLeod wanted to impress Lords of the Kings Court from Edinburgh so he invited them to a banquet at his 'room more lofty and a table more spacious' than they had, taking them to the flat-topped summit with light provided by his clansman, holding aloft flaming torches. The Lords were said to have been very impressed and spent some time at Dunvegan Castle. A less romantic view is that around 65 million years ago horizontal lava flows would have created these distinctive flat topped hills.

MACLEOD'S TABLE NORTH (HEALABHAL MHOR) WALK
Distance 4.5 miles with an estimated time of 4.5 to 5 hours.

A walk to the summit of one of the dominate feature of Duirinish, cloaked in myths and legends. The effort to negotiate the sometimes steep and pathless route is rewarded with truly magnificent views. Parking is roadside at grid reference 242 465 on the B884 single- track road from Dunvegan to Glendale. Please remember not to park in a passing place.

Begin with a short road walk back toward Dunvegan before taking the track on your right heading to the old settlement of Osdale appropriately named after Glen Osdale. Pass the refurbished cottages heading toward a burn, at this point the track deteriorates. The burn can be crossed by negotiating stepping stones, but good footwear is advisable to ensure your feet remain dry. Beyond the burn the route now follows sheep tracks across the heather-clad moorland heading toward the distant summit. The moorland is a delight with many species of wild flower to be found, sometimes in abundance.

As the summit gets closer, the slopes become much steeper and its does require selecting the easiest looking route, as there is no clear indication of the best line of ascent. Occasional ridges and outcrops of rock need to be overcome before reaching the base of the hill. The true base of the hill is a good place to rest a while and gaze in awe at the magnificent views with a chance to look back to the starting point to appreciate how much ascent has taken place.

The views to the north encompass Loch Dunvegan, the castle and the bright white sands of the Coral Beaches, Waternish and the distant Outer Hebrides. South east, the views overlook Loch Bracadale, and given the right weather conditions the distant Cuillin can also be seen. The final push to the flat-topped summit is very steep, mainly grassy but as with the lower slopes you need to devise your own route. Keep well to the left of the steep cliffs the drop from the summit. Finally, the mossy plateau comes into view for the first time, unlike most hills and mountains where the destination for most of a walk is clearly visible.

The route to the flat-topped summit is very steep, mainly grassy
and you will need to devise your own route.

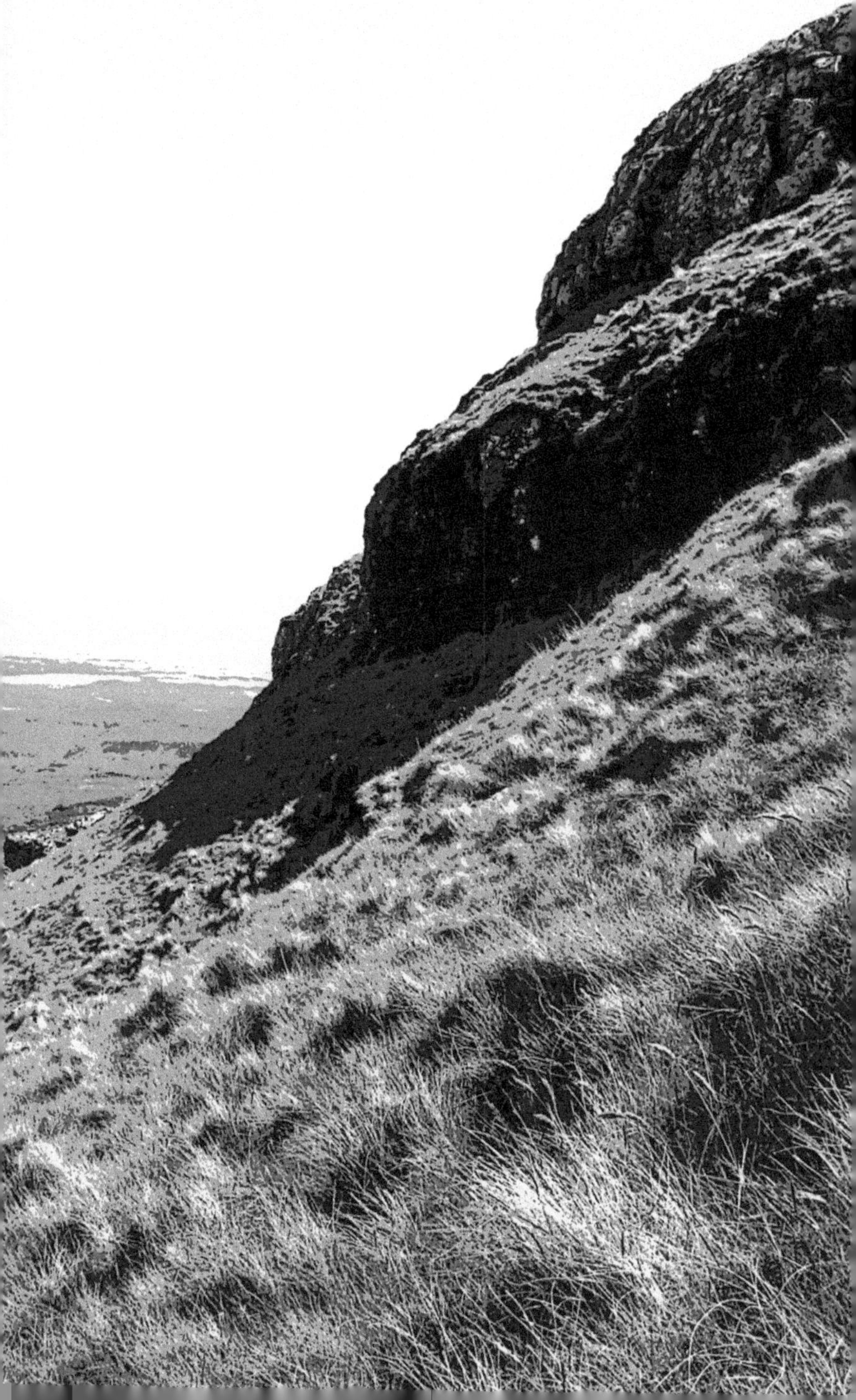

Head across the spongy flat-topped summit, keeping to the left of a lochan, to reach the large summit cairn where conformation is gained that the flat-topped summit of Healabhal Bheag away to the south is indeed the loftier of the two.

After spending a considerable amount of effort reaching the flat summit, no one would question staying some time to admire the magnificent vista from the top. A circumnavigation of the entire summit is essential to appreciate the entire panorama, but take care as the summit's mosses can be very wet at times and boggy ground is treacherous and needs to be avoided. Be prepared for a breezy reception aloft, for even on the calmest of days the winds at the summit can be quite invigorating.

The descent is taken by retracing your steps, again choosing your own route down, nevertheless made all the easier as you are now in full view of your destination. Although the walk to the summit and back looks reasonably easy, care needs to be taken as the upper slopes are very steep and may not be suitable for all, mists can also descend rendering the upper slopes very dangerous. The distance is not great, only 4 miles, but the going is hard at times; allow plenty of time for this walk to the lofty heights of Duirinish.

The single-track road continues north-westward where evidence of peat cutting can be seen.

PEAT CUTTING

Peat cutting normally starts in May, taking advantage of the more clement summer weather to dry the peat. Cut into brick shapes using a tool known as a peat iron, the bricks are then laid across the moor to dry for about three weeks before being stacked and turned. The peat iron was designed to cut lift and throw the peat in one movement. Vast areas of Skye are covered in deep layers of peat that continue to grow each year.

Crofters have a dedicated area of moorland where they are able to harvest the peat, used as household fuel in the Highlands for many centuries. Peat is formed in waterlogged, sterile acidic conditions that favour mosses, in particular sphagnum moss, as the plants die they are laid down and slowly build up as peat instead of decomposing due to the lack of oxygen in the bog.

Opposite page: A large cairn marks the summit of Healabhal Mhor.

MACLEOD'S TABLE NORTH
(HEALABHAL MHOR)

Working the peat bank

GLENDALE

Glendale sits north-west of Dunvegan accessible, only by the single-track road we are travelling along following the rugged shoreline of Loch Dunvegan, for most of the 10 miles a superb scenic journey. Glendale is made up from what are known as townships these being the small scattered settlements of Fasach, Feriniquarrie, Holmisdale, Lephin, Upper Milovaig, Lower Milovaig and Waterstein. The Glendale estate covers 23,000 acres, with its boundaries of Dunvegan in the east, Orbost in the south, and west to The Little Minch.

Close to The Hamara river lays the site of one of the original parish churches on Skye, Kilchoan Church. All that remains today are the foundation of this little church and the graveyard. The last service was said to have been held in the late 1700s. Tradition has it that the twisted elder tree that grows out of the little church was the site of the grave of a Scandinavian Prince known as Tiel, who came to grief in battle as his ship sailed into Loch Pooltiel, at that time known as Loch-a-Chuain.

Glendale beach looking along the loch out to The Little Minch and beyond to the outer isles. The calm sea reflecting the early morning sunlight. The rock in the foreground taking on an almost giant mouse appearance, could it be the Loch Pooltiel monster.I went back a few hours later to find it had gone but suspect that was something to do with the tide.

At the head of Loch Pooltiel we find Glendale beach where the Hamara River flows into the sea having risen some 6 miles south-east and 938 ft high upon the slopes of Beinn a Chapuill in the shadow of Healabhal Mhor. A ruined watermill is evidence of past industrial activity at Glendale, where for centuries the islanders used water power to mill their flour. During the 1970s the mill was fully restored complete with replica machinery of the type that would have been used during its heyday. Sadly, it has now fallen into disrepair the thatched roof having caved in.

The wildlife of Loch Pooltiel is varied with minke whales, seals and otters all being spotted. The tall cliffs, together with its many waterfalls, provide a spectacular backdrop, especially when viewed from the coast below Lower Milovaig where access to the shoreline is easily obtained. During stormy weather and particularly after heavy rain, the waterfalls are literally blown back up the cliffs, producing a fascinating spectacle. Glendale today is popular with tourists as the only route to Waterstein Head and Neist Point a further 3 miles west runs through Glendale. Many of the croft houses now serve as holiday accommodation for the growing tourist industry that caters for people seeking a holiday where you can find space and solitude amongst magnificent scenery.

Ahead of Glendale are the scattered settlements of Upper and Lower Milovaig set on a promontory overlooking Loch Pooltiel. The loch is home to Meanish Pier, once a busy port with steamers arriving from South Uist and Glasgow bringing coal and other supplies to this remote part of Skye; we are now some 50 miles from the old ferry crossing at Kylerhea. Cattle boats used the pier as the dropping off point at the start of a Drovers trail across Skye. Before the coming of the single-track road, this rough track would have provided the only access into Glendale aside from the sea.

Today, one period in the history of the Highlands is still very emotive, the Highland Clearances. Whole crofting communities were cleared by the mainly absentee landlords who decided sheep were more profitable than the rents paid by the crofters. The clearance came later to Skye in comparison to other areas of the Highlands, but it is estimated that during the 1800s over 80,000 people were forced to leave their homes in the Highlands, shipped overseas to other continents. Throughout Skye you will find the scattered remains of derelict communities, croft houses razed to the ground still returning to Mother Nature, a lasting reminder of a turbulent period of Highland history.

One such area to the west of Upper Milovaig is Lorgill, set above the shore of Moonen Bay with a distressing secret past belying its present serenity. Imagine if you can a settlement of ten families during the 1830s living in a small close-knit community seeking out a living from the land, having plentiful grazing for their livestock, the sea on their doorstep providing a rich harvest and fresh water from the burn, all the essential elements to maintain the family. Suddenly and without warning they were forced from their homes, taking only what they could carry, marched overland 20 miles to Loch Snizort to be transported overseas to Nova Scotia. Anyone over the age of 70 was refused passage and would have been sent to Glasgow to see out their remaining days in the poor house. Their houses were subsequently razed to the ground rendering them derelict.

The clearances continued well into the 19th century with the land given over to sheep and their tenant farmers transforming the Highlands into the landscape that we know today. Glendale became famous in the early 1900s when crofters became freeholders of the land they worked and lived on. The Glendale Martyrs had campaigned for decades to achieve their aim, and some endured imprisonment during the late 1880s. Among them was John MacPherson, eventually leading an uprising against their landlord. During the winter of 1883 a member of Glendale Estates trying to remove cattle was assaulted by the owners. Warrants were issued for their arrest with four policemen duly dispatched from Portree to Glendale. The police were met by a large crowd who subsequently overpowered them, hastening their retreat back to Portree.

A Royal Navy gunboat docked at Meanish Pier to arrest MacPherson and four other crofters to stand trial. It was agreed that Lord Napier would set up a commission to look into the grievances of the crofters, taking evidence he recommended some reform. By this time, the Highland Land league was increasing in membership with feelings running high, and subsequent rent strikes were to become common place across the Highlands and Islands. Prime Minister William Gladstone relented and eventually passed the crofters act of 1886, an act far more radical then Napier's reforms, giving the crofters security of tenure. The crofter's future was now secure with the croft passing to their heirs on death.

A memorial to the 'Glendale Martyrs' sits at the head of the Glendale road paying tribute to John MacPherson and his followers.

GLENDALE WATER MILL
(Ruins of)
Evidence of past industrial activity at Glendale where for centuries
the islanders used water power to mill their flour.

Glendale Shop and Post Office

Fresh milk and bread
Fresh and frozen meats
Local produce
Tinned goods
Household and cleaning products
Hardware and automotive goods
Wood and coal supplies
Papers and magazines
Stamps and stationery

Our opening hours are;
Winter (October through to May) : Monday to Saturday 11:00am to 6:00pm
Summer (June through to September) : Monday to Friday 10:00am to 7:00pm,
Saturday 10:30am to 7:00pm
We are closed on Sundays.

Located on the Duirnish peninsula to the North West of Skye, offering
many of the necessities for weekly grocery shopping, without having
to break your holiday or step out of the glen.
For enquiries regarding pre-packed welcome boxes
Telephone 01470 511266

WATERSTEIN HEAD WALK
Distance 2.5 miles with an estimated time of 2 - 2.5 hours

Waterstein Head stands proud amongst a chain of magnificent cliffs towering above the north-west coast of Duirinish in a line that extend for over 20 miles from Idrigill Point in the south culminating in the north at Biod an Athair, the tallest cliffs on Skye, rising sheer from the shore line to reach over 1,000 ft above sea level. This stretch of coast is amongst the most magnificent to be found anywhere in the British Isles. The walk, a relatively short one takes you to the trig point at the summit of Waterstein Head towering 970 ft above Moonen Bay with superb views west across The Little Minch to the Outer Hebrides over 20 miles distant.

Moonen Bay was once fished by Gavin Maxwell, author of *Ring of Bright Water*, for basking sharks from his base on the small island of Soay off the south-west of Skye close to Elgol. This is another there-and-back walk with a fairly steep ascent to a remote area of Skye. On the return journey views open up north to Biod an Athair (Skye Cliff) and the distant mountains of Harris. The walk begins at grid reference 146 488. Leave the road heading down toward the escarpment edge with Loch Mor set out below following the remains of an old dyke (turf wall). This provides easy walking, making use of sheep tracks. The walk soon turns to a gentle climb.

Head slightly away from the dyke to find a gap in the old fence. Shortly after the fence, you head for a small ravine crossing the burn. Continue to follow the dyke as it climbs steeply, and eventually Waterstein Head comes into view in the distance. Continue upward, where a rocky escarpment makes for a welcome place to sit and marvel at Neist Point and the lighthouse set out beneath, with the Outer Isles in the distance. (South Uist highest peaks Beinn Mhor over 2000 ft and Hecla appear remarkably close on a clear day are in fact 22 miles distant). On an overcast or misty day the outer Isles are hidden from view, but the walk should only be attempted when weather conditions are clear as the upper slopes follow close to a sheer drop. keep on the grass above the cliff which at this point becomes steeper, now following a fence on your left.

You will need to step over this fence and follow it upward, turning right to keep to the cliffs. To reach Waterstein Head go across to the top corner of the field where there is a trig point (997 feet). To the South are views to the waterfalls of Ramasaig Cliff and the distant Hoe. Return by the same route with the reward of distant views to the tallest cliffs on Skye across Loch Pooltiel to Biod an Arthair.

Waterstein Head from Moonen Bay.

NEIST POINT

NEIST POINT WALK
Distance 4.5 miles with an estimated time of 3.5-4 hours

Moonen Bay boasts some of the finest cliff scenery in Britain and Neist Point, our next destination, is no exception.

Both of these walks could be done on the same day; in reality both deserve to be undertaken on different days to fully appreciate the magnificent scenery, allowing one time to seek out the flora and fauna. Seals, killer whales and occasional young basking sharks can be spotted at sea. The birdlife is astounding with meadow and rock pipit, common buzzard, rough-legged buzzard, golden eagle, eider and long tailed ducks, and even occasional puffin have been spotted here while colonies of shags sit on the rocks far below the tall cliffs.

The quiet single-track road makes for a pleasing stroll before descending the steep escarpment to Skye's most westerly point. Set off at grid reference 132 478 at the end of the road.

There is no road access to Neist Point lighthouse and goods are taken down the steep incline by means of a hoist. If the hoist is operational take care, as the notice advises. Once past the winch at the foot of the steps continue through the gap crossing a wide grassy plateau before gaining height. The path follows the contours of the escarpment under the towering grassy slopes of An t–Aigeach, known locally as 'The Stallions Head'. On the seaward side the craggy rock face of An t-Aigeach rises 230 ft sheer from the sea and is home to a colony of gannets.

The views to your left become awe-inspiring across the sweep of Moonen Bay. The panorama encompasses Waterstein Head gently yielding to Ramasaig Cliff, the cliffs in turn fall steeply to Ramasaig Bay before gaining height culminating at The Hoe.

Since the opening of the Skye Bridge it has been said that Neist Point is nowadays the most westerly part of mainland Britain that one can access by road and on foot, some 13 miles further west than Lands End in Cornwall.

Neist Point lies some 13 miles further west than Lands End in Cornwall.
The path follows the contours of the escarpment under the towering
slopes of An t–Aigeach, known locally as 'The Stallions Head'.

NEIST POINT LIGHTHOUSE

The lighthouse stands 62 feet high with the light set 142 feet above the sea

The lighthouse has to withstand to worst that nature can yield as the most sever of Atlantic winter storms first make landfall on Skye at Neist Point. Completed in 1909, the lighthouse was fully manned right up until 1990. The light is the equivalent of 480,000 candles and has a nominal range of 16 miles, but it is said to be visible for over 20 miles. The lighthouse stands 62 feet high with the light set 142 feet above the sea.

In January 2005 the general lighthouse authorities came to a conclusion that the fog signal had a significantly reduced role in the modern marine environment, due to the use of electronic position finding aids and radar. The decision was taken that all fog horns were to be turned off, the last falling silent October 2005. Fog horns were first introduced to Scotland in 1876. When fog or mist rises the light becomes less visible and from a distance unseen. As with the light for identification, the sound from the fog horn was unique to the location.

The lighthouse buildings are now privately owned with no access available to the lighthouse. The walk to Neist Point has not always been straight forward as previous owners had restricted access to the path from the road.

Head for the jetty where numerous rock pools are teaming with aquatic life, including sea anemones, carnivorous marine animals that cling to the rocks. The reward for the effort is a small remote cove of white sand, similar to that found at the Coral Beaches, and black rocks pounded smooth by the relentless battering from Atlantic storms. Continue to the point rewarded with a view of Waterstein Head in the knowledge that you are now at the most westerly point of Skye.

The return is by retracing the outward journey, but a detour along the northern cliff edge will provide you with magnificent views back to the lighthouse and the sheer cliff face of An t-Aigeach, with a chance to get a closer look at the colony of gannets. Take care, as the exposed cliff face drops steeply away.

Continue across the grassy plateau, where once the lighthouse keepers would play golf, to reach the winch house. To rejoin the road from here requires a steep climb. A good excuse for a rest on the climb up the numerous steps is to look back and marvel at the panorama of Neist set out below with distant views to the outer isles.

As with most of Skye's promontories, our journey now continues by retracing the single- track road that brought us to our latest destination. Early travellers would describe this area beyond Glendale as being at the ends of the earth as the next landfall due west is America.

Opposite page: The path to Neist Point passes An t- Aigeach known as the Stallions Head. This sheer craggy cliff presents some of the hardest rock climbing on Skye.

NEIST POINT

An t-Aigeach towers above the path to Neist Point

The Blackface sheep is today the most common hill breed in Scotland, introduced into North Scotland in the early 19th century. Blackfaces are horned, with a black or black-and- white face and legs. Cheviot sheep whose wool was more valuable took their place for a while but now more popular as they can survive in the harsh climate of the hills and mountains of Scotland.

Past industrial activity can be seen close to the beach at Glendale.

Travelling back to Dunvegan we pass once again through Milovaig
and the shores of tranquil Loch Pooltiel.

LOCH DUNVEGAN

The tranquil shores of Loch Dunvegan are to be our close companion for the next 10 miles as the single-track road skirts the scenic loch for most of the return journey to Dunvegan, the seat of Clan MacLeod.

High above Dunvegan stands Duirinish Millennium Stone, erected by the people of Dunvegan to mark the year 2000. Taken from the shore of Strathaird in the south of Skye, the stone was transported using the same techniques that would have been used thousands of years ago. The stone was brought by boat then raised into position using manpower and wooden A frames. Standing 15 ft high and weighing 5 tons, the stone is set high above the old church at Dunvegan with commanding views to MacLeod's Tables and the distant Cuillin.

Glendale, Lower Milovaig and Loch Poolltiel.

DUIRINISH MILLENIUM STONE
DUNVEGAN

the three chimneys®

THE THREE CHIMNEYS
SERVING OUR GUESTS THE BEST OF SKYE, LAND AND SEA

The Three Chimneys Restaurant and The House Over-By are now open
seven days a week from mid January to mid December every year.
Lunch is served 12.15 - 1.45pm every day
Dinner is served 6.30 - 9.30pm every day
Reservations are essential.
To BOOK A TABLE or BOOK A ROOM please give us a call on
Telephone: 01470 511258 or
Email: eatandstay@threechimneys.co.uk
You can also visit our website at www.threechimneys.co.uk

raven press
gallery

The working studio of Kathleen Lindsley, wood engraver,
and Nick Carter, photographer.

Colbost   Dunvegan

Isle of Skye IV55 8ZS

Tel:01470511748(daytime) - 01470511367(evenings)

www.ravenpressgallery.co.uk

LOCH DUNVEGAN

ISLE OF SKYE

Wintry sun over Loch Dunvegan.
The main inhabitants of Skye enjoy a forage on the shore at low tide.

Dragonfly Studio

Skinidin
　Dunvegan
　Isle Of Skye
　IV55 8ZS

Tel: 01470 521505
www.dragonflystudioskye.co.uk

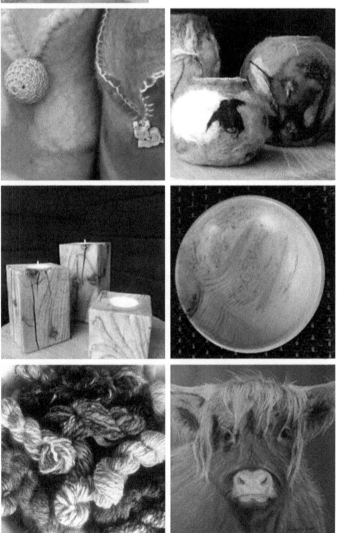

Our traditional family business combines
years of experience in handicrafts.

DUNVEGAN
CASTLE & GARDENS

Dunvegan Castle & Gardens has three craft and souvenir shops, the Gift Shop by the Castle car park, the Castle Shop inside the Castle itself and St Kilda Shop & Gallery by the Dunvegan Pier road near the village. All three shops offer an excellent range of high quality Scottish gifts and souvenirs to suit every taste from pottery, artworks, jewellery, books and postcards to our very own MacLeod of MacLeod Single Malt Scotch Whisky.

OPENING TIMES 1 April to 15 October
Daily 10am - 5.30pm (last entry 5pm)

DUNVEGAN CASTLE & GARDENS

According to their own genealogies, the MacLeods and Dunvegan became intertwined in the 13th century through the marriage of their progenitor, Leod, with the heiress of the Macarailts, in those days the Viking Seneschals of Skye who lived at Dunvegan. Leod himself was a son of Olaf the Black, King of the Isle of Man, who in turn was descended from the Norse king Harald Hardrada. Leod and his Lady had two sons, Tormod and Torquil, progenitors respectively of the MacLeods of Dunvegan, Harris and Glenelg and the MacLeods of Lewis. The gaelic word "Mac" meaning 'son of' helps to symbolise the moment when Clan MacLeod first appears as a historical reality.

Among all the historic houses of Scotland, there is none that for sheer manifold fascination overtops Dunvegan Castle. It is at once the greatest and most renowned among Hebridean strongholds, and the only one which has been continuously owned and (with the exception of the 80 years after the Potato Famine of the last century) occupied by the same family, during a period now reaching back over a span of very nearly eight centuries. Architecturally it is a structure of high importance, containing work of at least ten building periods. Its history, and that of the famous Clan whose Chiefs have ruled from their castled rock during all these many generations, is rich with drama and packed with colourful interest. Within Dunvegan's stately halls are priceless heirlooms, some of which have descended in the hands of the Chiefs of MacLeod since mediaeval times.

The castle is situated on an upstanding mass of partly columnar basalt, approximately 30 ft high, arising from the shores of Loch Dunvegan. Around it originally the sea ebbed and flowed. An important feature which gave Dunvegan Castle and those within its great strength was the existence of a fresh-water well. With this priceless resource added to the impregnability of its position, Dunvegan Castle presented a formidable obstacle to the enemies of the Chiefs of Clan Macleod.

Legends, however fantastic or far-fetched they may appear to be, are rarely without some trace of historical fact.

When a relic survives to tell its own story, that at least is one fact that is impossible to ignore. The precious Fairy Flag of Dunvegan, the most treasured possession of the clan, is just such a relic. The traditional tales about its origin, some of them very old indeed, have two themes - Fairies and Crusaders. Fairy stories are difficult to relate to fact; they often occur as a substitute for forgotten truth. The connection with the Crusades can, however, be linked to the only definite information available as to the origin of the Fairy Flag - the fabric, thought once to have been dyed yellow, is silk from the Middle East (Syria or Rhodes); experts have dated it between the 4th and 7th centuries, in other words, at least 400 years before the First Crusade. So was it the robe of an early Christian saint? Or the war banner of Harold Hardrada, King of Norway, killed in 1066, or did it emerge mysteriously from some grassy knoll in Skye? The legends are all we have to guide us to the answer.

'The Crusader version'.

A Macleod on a crusade to the Holy Land received food and shelter from a hermit in a dangerous mountain pass on the borders of Palestine. The Hermit warned him that an evil spirit, a destroyer of true believes, guarded the pass, but that with some advice and a piece of the True Cross, he might get through. The MacLeod slew the spirit, The Daughter of Thunder, "Nein na pheupere" and before she died she revealed to him the future of his Clan, directing him to take her girdle and make a banner of it and to make a staff of her spear.

'The Fairy Bridge version'.

Once upon a time a fairy married a Macleod Chief and was permitted to remain with him for 20 years before returning to fairyland. When the sad day came to part, the Chief took leave of his wife at the Fairy Bridge 3 miles from Dunvegan. She gave him the Banner, telling him that when he was hard pressed in battle, waiving it would bring a host of armed men to his side.

BONNIE PRINCE CHARLIE

Although the Chief at the time of the '45 did not support Bonnie Prince Charlie, many of his clan did do so. Visible from the castle on the other side of the Loch is Galtrigal, the home of the prince's pilot, Donald MacLeod of Galtrigal, the man who brought the prince 'Over the sea to Skye' from Uist during the time when the Prince was a fugitive. At the time the Chief was one of the people searching to apprehend the Prince. Flora MacDonald, the Jacobite heroine, was in the boat with the Prince, and equally being hunted by the MacLeod Chief.

By one of those quirks of fate, some twenty or thirty years later, her daughter had married the Tutor to the young Chief of MacLeod, and was living in the Castle. The mother, on one of her return visits from America where she had emigrated, is believed to have stayed for two or three years in the Castle and left her personal Jacobite relics to her daughter.

DUNVEGAN CASTLE

The magnificent stronghold of Clan MacLeod
reflected in the still waters of Loch Dunvegan

DUNVEGAN CASTLE & GARDENS
ISLE OF SKYE

Thus you will see in the castle still today her stays, her pin-cushion with the names of those who suffered in the '45, a Lock of the prince's Hair, a list of her children, and a small portrait of herself copied by the wife of the 24th Chief. Exhibited in the castle are also the Spectacles of Donald MacLeod of Galtrigal, the prince's boatman, and the Amen Glass which was given to Donald MacLeod by the prince, inscribed with the words 'To my faithful Palinurus', alluding to the boatman who conducts people across the Loch. Another interesting object with a fanciful engraving of the Prince is the tooth of a sperm whale, which can also be seen in the castle today.

The Clan MacLeod has survived down the centuries, surviving the extremes of feast and famine, the intermittent periods of warring with neighbouring clans, and the immense changes of social, political and economic life through which the Western Highlands and Islands have passed. Although three individual chiefs in the last seven generations have been comprehensively ruined by the apocalyptic difficulties caused by the unrelenting hostility from centralised government towards the Clan system practised behind the Highland line, the chief and his clans folk have remained faithful to Dunvegan Castle and the rock on which it stands. The 27th Chief was the first Chief to share his home with the public by opening it for charitable purposes two days a week in 1933. Since then the number of visitors has risen from a few hundred to tens of thousands. 'A visit to Dunvegan Castle provides one with an altogether fascinating and memorable experience'. The Castle gardens lie inland and are backed by mature woodlands. As the Isle of Skye is essentially made up of barren treeless moorland, these woods and gardens are like reaching a hidden oasis. The magnificent gardens provide considerable interest to many, following paths through woodland glades, past shimmering pools and burns fed by a cascading waterfall. The Castle Gardens were originally laid out in the 18th century, and considerable replanting and landscaping provides a legacy which current as well as future generations can enjoy and admire.

The tranquil waters of Loch Dunvegan are home to many islets, small uninhabited islands, and the knoll at Uiginish, its highest point a mere 140 ft above sea level. Uiginish Point is home to Uiginish beacon, a white plain structured tower just 16 ft high. The light flashes white, red, green every three seconds and can be seen from as far away as The Little Minch beyond Dunvegan Head, a distance of some 7 miles. Colonies of seals thrive on these uninhabited islets, and if you are lucky and the waters are calm you may just spot an otter or two.

Bonnie Prince Charlie had to leave Skye in a hurry, but you can stay for as long as you like to enjoy the varied wildlife of Loch Dunvegan and the spectacular views of the Outer Hebrides across the Little Minch. Seal boat trips depart from the pier below Dunvegan Castle using traditionally built clinker boats to visit the seal colony, where you can observe these playful sea mammals at close quarters. The knowledge of the boat men is second to none and you may see herons nesting as well as many other species of birds, including the arctic tern and the magnificent sea eagle.

LOCH DUNVEGAN
BOAT TRIPS TO VISIT THE SEALS ARE AVAILABLE
FROM THE CASTLE

COMMON SEALS

Loch Dunvegan provides a safe haven for a colony of common seals. The waters of the loch are shallow enough to prevent whales entering allowing the seals to bask in peace between feeding.

The seals will leave the sanctuary of the loch on the rising tide to feed in the fish-rich deeper waters of The Little Minch, returning to rest for several hours before setting out again to feed. Common seals have their pups during June, unlike the Atlantic seals who gives birth during autumn. The seals are a delight to watch, some becoming stranded with the ebbing tide on the higher rocks having to wait several hours for the tide to turn, before re-entering the water. Common seals are furry and can be seen leaping out of the water, much like a dolphin, to assist the fundamental process of moulting.

Over 90 per cent of the British population of common seals, also known as harbour seals, are to be found in Scotland. The common seals seen here on Loch Dunvegan feed further out to sea before returning on the ebbing tide to rest upon the rocks nourished on a variety of prey including sand eels, whitefish, herring, sprat and occasional octopus.

CORAL BEACHES WALK

Distance 4 miles with an estimated time of 3 hours.

A short coastal walk promising excellent views, leading to the bright white sands of the Coral Beaches. The walk starts at Claigan a remote group of crofts at the end of the single- track road leading north-west from Dunvegan. From the car park, the walk follows a track that gradually approaches the shore, first passing the small bay of Camas Ban. In bright sunshine the sands of the Coral Beaches are startlingly white, giving an illusion of a tropical island set against the azure sea.

This most gentle of walks begins at the car park grid reference 232 537. Pass through the kissing gate to follow a good track across a field. After a spell of wet weather the burn will need to be negotiated, but several stones make crossing easy. Pass through another gate to follow the track down to the shore. The small bay of Camas Ban is the first Coral Beach to be seen. I have heard it say that some visitors have thought this to be their destination, although at times of high tide very little of the beach is visible.

Carry on bearing slightly away from the coast to cross another burn, heading upward to a gap in the wall. A clear path continues, where in a short distance you are rewarded with the superb views to the main coral beach; if you have chosen a sunny day the azure seas and the bright white sands give an illusion of a tropical paradise.

Continue on toward the beach with easy walking over short turfs. On reaching the beach you will find that the sand is not true coral but comes from the bleached exoskeletons of the red seaweed Lithothanium Calcareum which grows in the shallow waters off shore. The red seaweed lays down an exoskeleton of chalk; when alive it is pink but becomes bleached white when dead. The steep sided Cnoc Mor a'Ghrobain that rises behind the beach is worth a climb, a mere 65 ft, a modest ascent compared to Skye's other coastal features, however your reward is a fine viewpoint. Dunvegan Head across Loch Dunvegan is clear to see, as are MacLeod's Tables and the distant outer isles.

During the summer months wildflowers are abundant on the grassy slopes and rocky outcrops of Cnoc Mor a Ghrobain. Having spent time admiring the views, move down to the shore and continue on around the rocky headland to Groban na Sgeire. To the north lie the Islands of Isay and Mingay. The wall running to the sea can be followed for a short distance, making use of sheep tracks above the rugged coast to view Lovaig Bay. Stein on the coast of Waternish is a mere 2.5 miles across the bay; however due to the characteristics of Skye's peninsulas to reach Stein does necessitate a 14 mile road journey back via Dunvegan. The topography does, though, provide for an exceptionally picturesque coastal journey.

The bright white sands of The Coral Beaches on a glorious sunny day, this could be anywhere in the Caribbean aside from the temperature.

The way back to the car park at Claigan is by retracing your steps, but why not spend some considerable time just sitting on the rocks or the beach listening to the shallow waters of Loch Dunvegan tumbling over the durable coral. On the return a slight deviation follows the rocky headland back to the main track. Keep to the seaward side where the path begins to rise as you leave the relatively flat foreshore, rejoining the track on the other side of the wall at Camas Ban. From here, follow the outward track back to the car park with views across Loch Dunvegan to the unmistakable MacLeod's Tables.

To continue our journey we now find ourselves travelling back through Dunvegan, all the while keeping a watchful eye on the loch, particularly if conditions are flat calm, the best opportunity to spot otters along the shore, feeding amongst the kelp. The next destination Waternish, Skye's smallest peninsula, is home to the oldest inn on Skye and the site of one of the most infamous of clan battles.

Wild flowers gain a precarious foothold on the rocky outcrop of Cnoc Mor Ghrobain.

HIGHLAND CATTLE

Highland cattle are a hardy breed that thrive where no other cattle could. They have the ability to make the best of poor grazing, are never housed, and have their calves outside.

They make great mothers breeding up to 18 years, are seldom handled and although normally docile should not be put in a position that could make them react. Cattle do not mix well with dogs and you should never try to touch them or come between mother and calf.

WATERNISH

One of Skye's smallest peninsulas, Waternish has a turbulent history, one involving clan feuds, massacres, and a significant period of de population resulting from the Highland Clearances. The peninsula is home to the oldest inn on Skye; the Stein Inn dating from the late 18th century.

Stein, nestling on the shores of Loch Bay, is a tiny hamlet accessed only by a single-track road that wends its way down to the sea. The most spectacular of sunsets unfold before you enhanced by the magnificent backdrop across Loch Bay of the small island of Isay, Ardmore Point and beyond to the Outer Hebrides.

Stein was originally built during the late 1700s as a fishing village, complete with houses for the fisherman and a pier. For a while it became the busiest fishing village on Skye but it seemed that the settlers could survive by living off the land, without having the need to spend time at sea. Now a picturesque seaside village, Stein was home for a while to the famous sixties singer Donovan.

It has been said that this is where Skye meets the sky and at times the Outer Hebrides running in an arch for over 130 miles from south to north feel almost touchable, even though they are over 25 miles distant.

As we leave behind yet another magical place our next destination takes us to one with a gruesome past, just over 4 miles north- west we come to the ruined church at Trumpan.

Beyond Trumpan there is nothing but cliffs and open moorland, apart from a small unmanned lighthouse at Waternish Point. There is a true feeling of remoteness about the promontory, although this has not always been so.

A cairn on the track to Waternish Point at grid reference 230 632 bears witness to another battle, built as a memorial to Roderick Macleod of Unish who died during clan battles with the MacDonalds of Trotternish around 1530. Unish was once a thriving settlement until the Highland Clearances, now all that remains are the sites of the ruined croft houses.

BONNIE PRINCE CHARLIE

Bonnie Prince Charlie, aided by Donald MacLeod and Flora Macdonald whilst escaping from South Uist, after defeat at Culloden in 1746 landed near Waternish Point. It is said that here they rested a while before continuing having been thwarted in an attempt to land at Ardmore Point, where during a storm where they were fired upon by soldiers.

Loch Bay from the shore at Stein. The settlement of Stein was built in the 1780s as a fisshing village. Once home to the sixties singer Donovan, Stein boasts some of the most dramatic sunsets on Skye.

STEIN INN
THE OLDEST INN ON SKYE

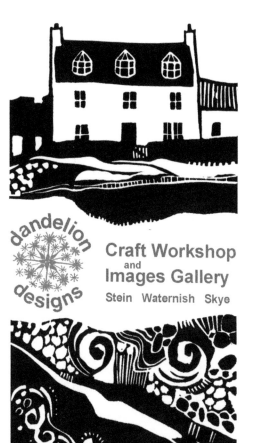

dandelion designs

dandelion designs

Craft Workshop
and
Images Gallery
Stein Waternish Skye

Original Arts and Local Handmade Craftwork

Easter to October open every day 11am - 5pm
(reduced hours in winter)   01470 592218
cathy@dandelion-designs.co.uk   www.dandelion-designs.co.uk

TRUMPAN OLD CHURCH

Here at Trumpan perhaps one of most cruel events in the islands sometimes brutal and bloody past was carried out at the Old Church. Trumpan's place in history was earned as a result of two massacres on the same day, a Sunday in May 1578. The chain of events had begun the previous year when Clan MacLeod found almost 400 MacDonald's hiding in a cave on the Isle of Eigg; the MacLeods suffocated them by entrapping them in the cave then setting light to the entrance.

On that fateful Sunday in 1578 the MacDonald's arrived from Uist by boat at Ardmore Bay below Trumpan. Under a veil of mist they came ashore unnoticed, moving to barricade the local population in the church. Seeking revenge for the massacre on Eigg they set fire to the thatched roof. The consequences of their actions resulted in the death of the entire congregation, aside from a small girl, who managed to escape to raise the alarm. Clan MacLeod arrived swiftly from Dunvegan where the flames had been seen to seek out revenge, and the MacDonald's never returned to Uist. Capturing the boats that by now were stranded in Ardmore Bay on an ebbing tide, they attacked and killed the MacDonald's, lining them up next to a turf dyke. The turf and stone wall was pushed over burying their bodies. To this end, the Battle of Trumpan is also referred to as the battle of the spoiled dyke.

The graveyard and ruins of Trumpan Church lie toward the end of the Waternish peninsula above Ardmore Bay, one of the most tranquil parts of Skye.

WATERNISH
ISLE OF SKYE
Where the most spectacular of sunsets unfold

Edinbane
Pottery
Workshop & Gallery

Specialists in both Woodfired and Salt Glazed Pottery

THE POTTERY IS OPEN THROUGHOUT THE YEAR
MONDAY to FRIDAY 9am - 6pm (7 days Easter - October)

t: 01470 582234
e: stuart@edinbane-pottery.co.uk
w: www.edinbane-pottery.co.uk

PORTREE

Our brief visit to Waternish ends back at the famous Fairy Bridge, we now head east, passing below the slopes of Ben Aketil, the site of the first wind farm on Skye. As we continue through several small settlements, the original single-track road is still visible at times to our left. On reaching Borve we turn right for a short distance to arrive at Portree, the islands capital. Portree takes its name from the Gaelic (Port-an-Righ) meaning Kings Port, named after King James V in 1540 as a consequence of his visit to the Highlands in an attempt to quell the clan battles of the time, although there is some dispute to this theory. Prior to this, the settlement was known as Kiltaraglen. Bonnie Prince Charles bade farewell to Flora MacDonald for the last time from Portree, while he was staying at MacNabs Inn, now known as The Royal Hotel.

In 1771 Portree had been developed as a fishing port by Sir James Macdonald. The port has witnessed numerous sad farewells, with countless sailings away from Skye particularly after the infamous potato famine of 1846 and the subsequent Highland Clearances that continued for the remainder of the late 1800s. During his visit to Skye in 1773, James Boswell made note that Mrs. Mackinnon told him *'Last year when the ship sailed from Portree for America the people on shore were almost distracted when they saw their relations go off: they lay down on the ground and tumbled and tore the grass with their teeth. This year there was not a tear shed. The people on shore seemed to think they would soon follow.'*

The natural setting for the harbour is enhanced by the coastal scenery and views to the Cuillin. Today used for fishing boats and pleasure craft, once used by steamers in the 1850s for several destinations including Glasgow and Stornoway. The brightly painted cottages that line the harbour have been featured on many calendars over the years similar to the famous harbour side of Tobermory. Located on the southern outskirts of Portree you will find the Aros Centre, Skye's visitor centre, which includes an innovative exhibition on the history of the island.

The quayside Portree.

The harbour once used by steamers in the 1850s is today used for fishing boats and pleasure craft.

Overleaf: Brightly painted cottages adorn the harbourside at Portree.

Portree
Isle of Skye

Port Rìgh

An t-Eilean Sgitheanach

TIPPECANOE GALLERY & GIFTS

PORTREE

TIPPECANOE

Tippecanoe is a contemporary gift shop & gallery situated in the
island capital Portree, bursting with bright ideas for
gifts & souvenirs to make you smile.

www.tippecanoe.co.uk

THE SKYE MUSEUM OF ISLAND LIFE

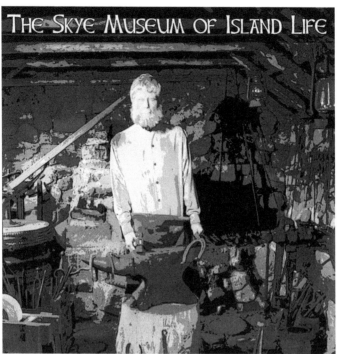

KILMUIR - TROTTERNISH - IV51 9UE
Opening times: Easter - October
Monday - Saturday 9-30am to 5pm

Telephone 01470 55220   www.skyemuseum.co.uk

The Skye Museum of Island Life at Kilmuir, was opened in 1965. The aim was to preserve a township of thatched cottages, each one depicting, as closely as possible, the conditions prevailing on the island at the close of the nineteenth century.

TROTTERNISH

Leaving behind the island capital, we now take the main A87 heading once again north to the most mystifying and surreal of Skye's peninsulas, Trotternish. The largest landslip to have occurred in Britain has created a 20 mile inland cliff, the Trotternish Ridge. We skirt the waters of Loch Snizort Beag, a loch that saw numerous sad farewells from these shores during the Highland Clearances. We pass Kingsburgh where Bonnie Prince Charlie spent the night having earlier landed on Skye close to Monkstadt with Flora MacDonald.

As the main port of Uig comes into view all is not as it seems. Overlooking Uig Bay at South Cull we find resembling a Norman Tower, Captain Fraser's folly dating from the 1890s. It is said the captain was a notorious landlord and the folly was once used as a collection point for the crofters to pay their rent. The tower is now empty, no longer inhabited since the 1950s, although plans are under way to restore the tower for residential use once again.

Below is the small port of Uig, the ferry terminal to Lochmaddy, North Uist and Tarbert on the Isle of Harris. Before reaching the port, a single-track road on our right begins to climb, negotiating a hair-pin bend to reach a fork in the road. The right fork would take us across the backbone of Trotternish to reach the ridge, while the left will skirt the west coast to reach Kilmuir the location of the Skye Museum of Island life and Duntulm, home to a ruined castle, our two next ports of call.

Common Cottongrass is a member of the sedge family growing on wet moorland and in boggy pools, a distinctive feature of the landscape of Skye. The flower head is an inconspicuous brownish colour that develops during the early summer into balls of long cotton like hairs.

UIG
ISLE OF SKYE
Travel by Ferry to the Western Isles

KILMUIR

At Kilmuir we seem to have travelled back in time as we approach a crofting settlement from the 19th Century; it is in fact the Skye Museum of Island Life. Before visiting the museum, we continue a short distance past the entrance to perhaps the most iconic tribute on Skye, a monument to the memory of Flora MacDonald.

Flora was staying with her uncle on South Uist in the Outer Hebrides when Bonnie Prince Charlie sought refuge after fleeing from the defeat at Culloden. With a huge bounty on his head, time was running out for Charlie who, having been tracked down to Uist, Flora agreed to help smuggle the Prince to Skye, dressed as her maid Betty Burke. They set off in an open boat running into a storm off Ardmore Point, coming under fire from soldiers they were forced to find shelter for a while in a cave at Waternish Point, eventually arriving at Monkstadt, spending one night at Kingsburgh ahead of reaching Portree a day later. As they parted the Prince gave Flora a lock of his hair, she kept one of the sheets that the Prince had slept in later to be used as her shroud.

Flora was arrested and imprisoned for a while in the Tower of London for her help in Prince Charlie's escape but released under the Act of Indemnity 1747, later marrying Allan MacDonald of Kingsburgh in 1750. Sailing to live in America in 1774, Flora eventually returned to Skye after the War of Independence. Flora died in 1790. It is said that 3,000 mourners attended the funeral. The Celtic cross in the graveyard at Kilmuir was erected in 1880 and engraved are the words of Dr Johnson.

FLORA MACDONALD Preserver of PRINCE CHARLES EDWARD STUART
'Her name will be mentioned in history and if courage
and fidelity be virtues, mentioned with honour'

SKYE MUSEUM OF ISLAND LIFE

A hundred years ago thatched houses were very much a part of the Highland scene and within their walls, by the light of the peat fire, the crofters of the Islands kept alive the songs and stories which have made the Hebrides famous throughout the world. Warm, sturdy and economical of scarce materials, the croft house was admirably suited to the landscape and the climate. It embodied the principles of streamlining hundreds of years before scientists thought of the idea, with the result that it could stand up to the worst of winter gales.

SKYE MUSEUM OF ISLAND LIFE
KILMUIR
ISLE OF SKYE

As their number fast diminish, it is appropriate that a few should be preserved; and it was with this in mind that a group of old thatched buildings was set aside as a museum.

The first cottage to be opened to the public in 1965 was the dwelling house, which dates back to the mid-19th century. This cottage is a good example of the typical Skye house of that era, when houses on the island, with very few exceptions, were of this standard and type. By present-day standards the old Highland house was basic and crude but nevertheless, it was adequate in its own day and gave shelter and warmth to men and women who spent most of their time out of doors and cared little about worldly possessions or domestic luxury.

The museum is built around a reconstructed small crofing village, on display almost everything that such a township on Skye would have contained over a cenyury ago.

When a house was being planned, the first requisite was the finding of a suitable stance and, needless to say, a spot near a well was preferred since all the water for the household had to be carried by hand in buckets. The availability of stones was also a major consideration, and if enough stone could not be found near at hand the sitting of the house could suffer. On a treeless island such as Skye, the finding of suitable timber for the roof could also present a problem. Driftwood was often all that could be found. Before the era of lighthouse development and in the days of wooden ships, shipwrecks were quite a common occurrence, often providing a Godsend, as timber in abundance was cast upon the shores.

The type of cottage to be found on Skye was built with walls up to three feet in width and beating a hip-ended roof with over-hanging eaves of thatch, which formed a fringe around the wall top. The roof was constructed on the couple and purlin system, with rafters of rough, round timber. Light branches laid neatly over the purlins carry the 'divots' or turf squares which were neatly tiled to form a bed for the thatch. The thatch used on Skye was common rush or locally grown reeds.

As one enters the croft house (the largest in the group) the room to the right is the kitchen, and here the family cooked, ate and sat - it was the main room in the house. All the cooking was done on the peat fire which burned day and night, summer and winter on the open hearth. Heavy pots of cast iron were used, and the three legged pot was often to be suspended over the flame by means of the 'swee'. The cruise, a lamp burning fish liver oil was used before paraffin lamps became common. The crockery in the home was displayed on the shelves of the dresser and it was customary to display coronation memorabilia and other artefacts on a prominent shelf. The furniture consisted mainly of a bench or settle, a table, a barrel chair by the fireside for the 'man of the house', and another two or three chairs or stools for the family or the visitor.

On a mantelpiece one would always find a Gaelic bible and a family photograph if such was available. No Highland cottage was complete without a set of bagpipes, a fiddle or a Jew's harp. These items were indeed necessities, as crofting families had to depend entirely on their own resources. The father was often able to teach his sons the art of playing some instrument, and how better could one pass a winter evening than in the happy atmosphere of Gaelic songs, music and discussion around a cosy peat fire?

There can be few parts of the world, if any, which have such a wide and varied culture as the Highlands and Islands of Scotland, and in their language, song and music they have a great deal of which to be proud.

THE CEILIDH HOUSE

The word Ceilidh means a small homely gathering of friends. Before the arrival of radio and television, it was customary for neighbours to meet together during the long winter evenings to make their own entertainment. Songs were sung, stories were told and discussion on many and varied topics took place.

Young and old engaged in the congenial proceedings, and as they sat happily around the peat fire the long dark night soon wore away, leaving with each and all a sense of the close community spirit and atmosphere, that was once so characteristic of the islands of the Hebrides. James Boswell, in an account of his visit to Skye along with Dr. Johnson in 1773, describes a house in which they stayed in south Skye. He states: 'We had no rooms that we could command, for the good people here had no notion that a man could have any occasion but for a mere sleeping place'

THE OLD SMITHY

A smithy could be found in every community in the past, but today the function is no longer required in rural crofting areas, mechanisation has long since taken over from the good and faithful workhorse. The smithy was a very popular meeting place for the local folk, young and old alike. The smith was never to be found alone, and all the happenings of the place were discussed in his hearing by those who called in. Farriery was the mainstay of the smith's income. Every crofter had a horse, or sometimes two, and in the busy seasons of spring and summer there was always a horse in the smithy being shod. In winter the smith was never idle and was always at his anvil making horseshoes or mending the many various items sent to him for repair.

THE WEAVERS COTTAGE

The small cottage could often be seen as a very busy workshop. The village weaver could always find plenty of work to keep the shuttle going, producing not only the tweed for all types of garments but also for blankets and plaids. The old handloom on display at the museum is over 100 years old and is typical of the type used in homes of the Highlands before automatic looms were introduced. The old barn completes the crofting community.

SKYE MUSEUM OF ISLAND LIFE
KILMUIR

The bellows ensured the peat fire burnt continually, day and night, winter and summer.

Leaving the past behind, we head north-east to Duntulm, our journey taking us through a dramatic boulder-strewn landscape set below the 300 ft towering mass of Bealach Lochdarach, travelling along a rugged sweep of coastline.

DUNTULM CASTLE to RUBHA HUNISH WALK
Distance 4.75 miles with an estimated time of 3 hours

A spectacular coastal walk draped with a turbulent history, visiting the ruined castle at Duntulm and the abandoned township of Erisco. The walk takes you above the northern- most point of Skye, Rubha Hunish, a remote promontory made more so as the only access is by negotiating the precarious descent of the 300 ft high cliffs of Meall Tuath guarding over the headland.

The route to this northern most point begins following the rocky shoreline with the return taking advantage of the distant views to the Trotternish Ridge from the heather clad hillsides above the abandoned crofts of Erisco.

Park on the roadside close to the castle at grid reference 410 740. A visit to the ruined castle is probably best taken before the walk as most of the route can be seen from the castle walls. Go through the gate to reach the castle sat proudly on a rocky promontory overlooking Tulm Bay. Once and Iron Age Broch the site of Duntulm Castle has also been used as a Viking stronghold before being occupied by the MacLeods in the 14th century. The castle was later inhabited by the MacDonalds, who were known as The Lords of the Isles. The MacDonald's enlarged the structure during the 17th century.

Duntulm Castle, guarded on three sides by sheer cliffs, dates from the Iron Age when it was first used as an Iron Age Broch, history suggests that it became a Pictish fort before becoming the stronghold of the Vikings. James V of Scotland visited the castle in 1540 during his journey around the Highlands, attempting to bring to an end the feuding between local clans. The castle was eventually abandoned in 1730. Documentary evidence from 1880 suggests that the castle once stood several storey's high. Very little now remains of the original 17th century structure, the disrepair augmented by a storm in 1980 that felled one of the last remaining masonry walls. Some of the castle stonework is reputed to have been used for local building in the past.

The Castle is said to be haunted by several past inhabitants, including Hugh MacDonald who was imprisoned and left to starve to death in the dungeon for an attempt to take the land belonging to the MacLeods, legend has it that he was driven mad and tried to eat his hands before dying. Another legend tells of a nursemaid who is said to wander through the ruined castle, having been killed for accidentally dropping the baby boy of the Clan Chief from a castle window onto the rocks below. She was holding him aloft for the Chief returning from a voyage at sea. This tragic accident and subsequent haunting were cited as the reason for the abandonment of the castle.

Return to the single-track road turning left to initially gain height. Once the road begins to descend the former coastguard cottages come into view with a small loch beyond. Before reaching the cottages at a bend in the road, take the track down to the sea.

Continue down the track to the coast below the castle to follow the rocky shoreline heading in the direction of the distant headland of Meall Tuath. The grassy foreshore makes for easy walking, with the delightful rocky coastline frequently tempting you to the water's edge.

Once and Iron Age broch the site of Duntulm Castle has also been used as a Viking stronghold before being occupied by the MacLeods during the 14th century.

Thrift flowers freely on the rocky outcrops during the summer months, more commonly known as sea pink, it is abundant throughout Skye during late spring and early summer, producing a wonderful displays of colour. In contrast to the beautiful displays of wild flowers, a fascinating variety of seaweed can be found, clinging to the rocks between high and low water. At the point where the shore meets the lower slopes of Meall Tuath you are forced inland gaining height by crossing a stile. The area is sometimes boggy but is covered with sporadic crops of cotton grass dancing in the gentlest of breezes during the summer months. The upper slopes are clad in heather and gorse until the highest ground is reached where walking is now on short turfs.

Thrift, more commonly known as sea pink, is abundant on coastal rocks throughout Skye during spring and early summer producing a wonderful display of colour. Thrift can also be seen growing on the slopes of the higher regions of Skye somehow growing from what appears just a small crack in the rock.

Once the higher ground is attained, you are rewarded with magnificent views to the northern most point of Skye. Rubha Hunish is set out below like a giant map with the distant islands of Gearran, Gaeilavore and Fladda-chuain, where the remains of a chapel dedicated to St Columba can be found, rising from the waters of The Little Minch some three miles off shore. During November 2002 HMS Trafalgar, a 4,750 tonne nuclear submarine ran aground during a training exercise on the uninhabited craggy rocks off Fladda-chuain, with the damage estimated to have cost in the region of £5 million. On the horizon can be seen the Isle of Harris, some 16 miles distant.

The view north west across Tulm Bay to Tulm Island takes in the distant remote small isles of Gearran, Gaeilavore and Fladda-chuain.

The descent to Rubha Hunish from Meall Tuath is to be found almost concealed behind a large rocky outcrop at the edge of the towering cliffs. The route down is severe for the first part and may not be to the liking of all, so it might be as well to admire the outstretched promontory from above. The views from the basalt-columned cliffs are some of the best to found in Britain.

Soon the old coastguard hut comes into view, complimenting the landscape, its bright white walls reflecting the summer sun set against the azure background 300 ft above the sea. The former coastguard building overlooking The Little Minch would have been initially manned around the clock. The coastguard hut has been fully restored after suffering severe damaged during the great storm of January 2005, now used by The Mountain Bothies Association. The association is a charity looking after almost 100 shelters in some of the more remote parts of the British Isles.

Perhaps the best views of the basalt-columned cliff face can be gained if you have resisted the descent to Rubha Hunish by continuing along the cliff top to the right of the old coastguard hut.

The return part of the walk begins here if you can tear yourself away from the views. Maintain a south-south-east direction following the sheep tracks over heather-clad turfs always above but toward the deserted crofts of Erisco, keeping the sea and Tulm Island on your right.

The path keeps to the hillside, crossing a stile where you can drop down to take a closer look at the abandoned township. The crofts of Erisco were unusual in that they were built along a straight line, similar to the crofts on the remote islands of the St Kilda archipelago, a group of islands some 41 miles west of the Outer Hebrides. The crofters must have found it very hard to leave when the area was cleared as they had good grazing and easy access to the sea. Climb back to the escarpment to continue south-eastward heading all the while for the sheep pens.

Rubha Hunish from Meall Tuath the most northerly point on Skye. Three miles off shore lay the small islands of Gearran, Gaeilavore and Fladda-chuain.

The northern-most extent of the Trotternish Ridge, Sgurr Mor stands over 1,600 ft above sea level and dominates the distant landscape looking south-east from the track above Erisco. Continue following the sheep paths where posts indicate the way, keeping the sheep pens on your right. Go through the gate to turn right to gain the road, passing the phone box. A short period of easy road walking will bring you to the delightful Loch Cleat and the former coastguard cottages at Duntulm. The single-track road continues upward past the hotel before descending back to the start of the walk.

The spectacular Trotternish Ridge is an inland cliff that runs for almost 20 miles, winding its way along the spine of the peninsula from Portree in the south to its northern extent. The ridge is made up of several pinnacles and peaks set against a backdrop of steep cliff faces. The most notable of the pinnacles is the Old Man of Stoor, appearing to be precariously balanced on the slopes of The Stoor. The pinnacle is spectacular and can be seen from many vantage points and stands over 160 ft high, a fascinating sight that awaits as we head southward down the east coast of Trotternish.

Go through the gate to turn right to gain the road passing the phone box.

STAFFFIN BAY

Leaving behind the most northerly part of Skye, we now return south-east to find Staffin Bay and the coastal settlement of Staffin, 'The Place of Pillars'. The name originates from the Vikings referring to the basalt columns of the cliffs. The Jurassic rocks of this coast have revealed a fascinating insight into the past, with an impressive array of dinosaur remains being discovered. At Corran, fossilised dinosaur footprints can be found at low tide, although at times they are buried beneath the sand. It is believed that the leader of Staffin sent a message to John MacPherson of Milovaig during the period of unrest telling him to 'stretch the law but do not break it'. At Staffin a single-track road forks right, leading to the small settlements of Marishader and Garros. Marishader was the home to the Martins of Marishader, made famous in Skye's history for Martin Martin author of *A Description of The Western Isles*.

Staffin takes its name from the Viking 'The Place of Pillars' named after the basaltic columned cliffs.

KILT ROCK
Close to Kilt Rock Mealt Waterfall fed from Loch Mealt
freefalls into the Sound of Rassay 170 ft below.

Legend has it that the two stone pillars standing on the moor near to Garros mark the site where two foolish brothers were said to have fought to the death for an inheritance.

A mile out of Staffin we come across Loch Mealt and a most impressive waterfall close to Kilt Rock. The spectacular rock formation known at Kilt Rock takes its name from the massive columns of dolerite, giving the appearance of pleats in a tartan kilt. Although not identical, they are similar to the basalt rocks at Staffa near Iona that are said to have been formed over 55 million years ago. Mealt waterfall at grid reference 508 655 has the splendid backdrop of Kilt Rock, fed by Loch Mealt, the water freefalling into the Sound of Raasay 170 ft below.

THE TROTTERNISH RIDGE

The vast inland cliff was formed around 50 million years ago when over 20 layers of volcanic rock were laid down, the sedimentary rocks which had been covered by the flows of basalt lava eventually collapsed under the weight. The result of this huge landslip, the largest in the British Isles, was the creation of the most spectacular, surreal landscape we see today.

Most of the ridge is easily accessible, with the majority of the walking on turf paths. The whole route can be walked in two days, but the area can be treacherous, with mists seemingly descending from nowhere that have been known to last for several days.

The ridge is traversed by a single-track road linking Staffin with the main port to the western isles, Uig. To the north of the single-track road is the Quiraing with the imposing cliffs of Meall na Suiramac over 1,700 ft above sea level. Opposite the tall cliff is a massive rock known as The Prison, an almost sheer face on one side and very steep grassy slopes on the other. The Needle, The Table and several other striking features bedeck the area, the ridge providing breathtaking views over Staffin Bay and across the sea to Wester Ross.

The most famous landmark on Skye has to be the Old Man of Stoor, the final goal in our journey exploring the misty isle, perhaps the most mysterious and eerie destination on Skye, perched below the tallest part of the ridge. The Stoor has featured in many TV and film productions, among these the 1975 film *The Land That Time Forgot* and the television series *Hamish Macbeth*.

The Trotternish Ridge runs for over 20 miles.

Skyelight CANDLES

SKYELIGHT CANDLES
STAFFIN on the TROTTERNISH RIDGE
Open Easter week until the end of October
Telephone 01470 562738

www.skyelight.co.uk

THE STOOR
TROTTERNISH RIDGE From LOCH FADA
ISLE OF SKYE

Looking north toward the Quiraing. The imposing cliffs of Meall na Suiramach with the ridge height of over 1,700 ft and opposite the massive rock known as The Prison with an almost sheer face on one side and very steep grassy slopes on the other.

THE OLD MAN OF STOOR WALK
Distance 3 miles with an estimated time of 3-3.5 hours

A colossal pillar undercut at the base standing over 160 ft high set below the towering Stoor, an inland cliff 2,360 ft above sea level, the Old Man is by far the most famous of the pinnacles and peaks that abound in this area of Trotternish. The Old Man was first climbed in 1955 by the late Don Whillans, being graded a very severe climb.

The steep but easily navigable route leads you into the sanctuary (Coire Faoin), flanked by the pinnacles and pillars set beneath the ridges highest point. When mists descend and melt away from the summits in a short space of time it creates a constantly changing eerie atmosphere that adds to this mysterious place.

Park in the lay-by at grid reference 508 528 on the Portree to Staffin road. Go through the gate where detailed information about the Stoor can be found, then follow a clearly defined path up through the forest. The first part of the climb is quite steep in places with no extended views, although the path having been rebuilt by the Skye and Lochalsh Footpath Trust makes for relatively steady progress. As you continue to climb higher, look for breaks in the trees providing tantalising views across the Sound of Raasay, and onward to the mountains of Applecross on the mainland.

As you leave the forest behind pass through a gate and look up in awe at the massive inland cliffs of The Stoor. Depending on the light, you may need to look a second time to pick out the Old Man and the other pinnacles as they can merge into the background. A few seconds of concentration, though, and they will soon become foremost features in the midst of this surreal landscape.

The path climbs ever higher and closer to the strange pinnacles and peaks, with a variety of tracks available to reach our goal. With the view now spread out behind you, a section of well-laid stone path branches off to your left, at first taking you away from the Old Man as it climbs steeply, soon to circles its way back in the right direction. Stop for a while and marvel at the view behind you to Loch Leathan and Loch Fada, their waters supplying the small hydro-electric power station below the cliffs on the shore at Bearreraig Bay.

The path snakes its way around the contours ever upward until you reach the foot of the Old Man. You are now in a surreal world, with the sanctuary set below and above the dark, craggy unstable cliff face of The Stoor, while to the north of the Old Man stands Needle Rock.

Coire Faoin, the sanctuary should not be missed. Follow the sheep tracks down to take in the tranquil atmosphere only broken occasionally by the distinctive call of ravens circling overhead. The view back to the Old Man perhaps may enlighten you as to the origin of its name, one theory goes that he lost his head in a storm in the late 1800s, while others differ, but I will leave that to your imagination. How long you remain here before setting back on the return only time will tell, but what is certain are the pinnacles and pillars create a unique landscape of beauty and mystery.

The Old Man can be circumnavigated but only if you are reasonably confident to do so and should never be attempted in bad weather as mists will belie the hidden dangers.

The descent can be taken using one of several paths that lead you to the gate ahead of re- entering the forest. The views on the return part of this walk are on par with any we have been privileged to witness throughout Skye, Raasay extended before you from a shimmering sea and on the horizon the mountains of Wester Ross.

The Cuillin, some 20 miles to the south, and the distant shores of Lochalsh can be seen on a clear day. The going is easier as you begin the descent into the wood watching for rabbits that seem to forage without a care in the world as you pass by.

The dense canopy of the conifer plantation is slowly being replaced with a return to planting of more native species.

Continue downhill through the forest back to the car park.

Alas, we have now reached the end of our journey exploring the misty isle. For those who are privileged to know this beautiful island intimately, there are many places we have not visited, indeed there is nowhere on this enchanting island that is not deserving of a visit. What I have tried to achieve on the journey is to provide an insight for the visitor, and in particular the first-time visitor, to make possible an extensive array of coastal, mountain and historical sites that could be visited in a week. I would though, recommend any one planning to visit this beautiful island to stay a wee while longer. The walks featured range from a very easy stroll taking in the Coral Beaches to the more strenuous route to Camasunary, but like most things the reward is well worth the effort, particularly when Camasunary comes into view for the first time.

The diversity of Skye's weather with all its changing moods, crystal-clear light generates a paradise for photographers. Yes, it does rain and the wind blows strong at times, but as the saying goes on Skye wait a short while and the sun will shine again. The weather is an important constituent to the dramatic scenes that unfold before you.

I have included brief notes on the islands sometimes turbulent past, although it is not a thoroughly detailed history, I hope it has helped to provide you with an emotion of what makes this island so special.

I trust you have enjoyed the journey and it will inspire you to visit Skye. You are assured of a warm welcome at any time of year. During the summer, Skye is blessed with long hours of daylight, so why not come 'over the sea to Skye' in the traditional way, by ferry from Glenelg. Come to the island in winter where both the wild stormy days and tranquil frosty ones will inspire you, the winter sun to be found low in the sky, creating perfect light for the photographer.

Thank you for joining me on this wonderful journey.

THE OLD MAN OF STOOR
TROTTERNISH
ISLE OF SKYE

FLORA MACDONALD

FLORA MACDONALD Preserver of PRINCE CHARLES EDWARD STUART
'Her name will be mentioned in history and if courage
and fidelity be virtues, mentioned with honour'

BONNIE PRINCE CHARLIE

This painting is the only one of Charles known to have been painted in Britain.
The painting was intended to be taken to England and used as the basis for an
official royal portrait once Charles had ascended to the throne.

CORAL BEACH ISLE OF SKYE
The shells and seaweed have been
arranged to create a picture.
But is it art ?

USEFUL INFORMATION

Mallaig Ferry to	01687 462403
Armdale (Skye)	01471 844248
Uig Ferry (Skye) to	01470 542219
Tarbert (Harris)	01859 502444
Lochmaddy (North Uist)	01876 500337
Glenelg - Kylerhea Ferry	07881 634726

Crossing time 5 minutes.
No reservation required
Easter-October only

Rail Kyle of Lochalsh	01599 534824

Police / Mountain Rescue	Emergency 999
Portree	01478 612888
Broadford	
Dunvegan	Non urgent 101
Uig	

Hospital

Portree	01478 613200
Broadford	01471 822491

Doctors

Portree	01478 612013
Broadford	01471 822460
Carbost	01478 640202
Dunvegan	01470 521203
Sleat	01471 844283

Petrol
Portree
Broadford (24 hours)
Dunvegan
Uig

Lightning Source UK Ltd.
Milton Keynes UK
UKHW020811060922
408371UK00006B/346

9 781367 565999